Straight Course

Speed Skiing in the Sixties

Dick Dorworth on his reord run, Portillo Chile

The Straight Course

Speed Skiing in the Sixties

Dick Dorworth

WESTERN EYE PRESS

THE STRAIGHT COURSE
is published by
WESTERN EYE PRESS,
a small independent publisher
(very small, and very
independent) with a home
base in the Colorado
Rockies and an office in
Sedona Arizona.
The Straight Course *is also*
available as an eBook
in various formats.

© *2011 Dick Dorworth*
Dick welcomes your feedback.
You can write him at
dorworth@mindspring.com

Western Eye Press
P O Box 1008
Sedona, Arizona 86339
1 800 333 5178
www.WesternEyePress.com

First edition, 2011
ISBN 978-0-941283-31-1

Back cover 2011 author's photo
by Carolyn Woodham.

Looking up the speed track, Portillo

BOOK ONE

Portillo
1963

Memoires — Dick & C. B. Vaughn, Portillo 1963

CHAPTER ONE

Some off-snow education

GROWTH AND LIFE DO NOT ABOUND at high elevations of the Andes Mountains. In the thin, pure atmosphere existence is lean, in some respects the correspondence of desert. Man, who is everywhere, brings the living that is his to the mountains, his toys and tools, wars and religions, games and faith. In winter he sees snow mice scamper from somewhere to somewhere else and he forgets about them. He sees wild dogs and his instincts remembers more than his brain. He sees the giant winged condor soaring high above. He feels awe. He wonders.

He wonders about.....what? His own nature? God? Truth? Separateness? Freedom? One of man's groping in darkness to describe and see light, to understand and communicate, but in the end it is an incommunicable, individual matter.

I discovered an inner value in the Andes and recognized it immediately. The moment of my self-detection occurred in springtime September, 1963 at the Chilean ski resort Portillo. The action which unfogged that particular mirror involved an attempt to set a world speed record on skis.

It was a successful attempt. The record was gained, the dream fulfilled, the point proved. That should have ended the story, but stories only end for convenience and life is seldom as tidy and convenient as the stories men tell about it. The writer writes to the form. The voice of the raconteur grows tired. The balladeer sings her song. The barroom philosopher drinks his fill and falls asleep. The poet leaves his message.

3

There is no ending and beginnings are arbitrary points in time.

This is a groping in the darkness of white paper and blank computer screen to describe my experience in what I call "the big speeds." It touches upon friendship and love and man's hereditary hunger for putting his life on the line every so often.

Al "Tiger" Jackson was a middleweight boxer around Reno in the 1950s. He was pretty good, but I once watched him throw a fight so obviously that I laughed right through my teen age vision of pure sport. Tiger was Negro. I didn't meet him until Spring, 1962 when he was working on Reno's garbage trucks.

We met in Henry's Corner Bar on the corner of Lake Street and Commercial Row and I was with Dana. Tiger had a beautiful white smile in a square jaw and he laughed at the world and at men who spent their time dancing with the whores at Henry's. He laughed with them as well, but he was too tired from Reno's garbage for dancing.

He called us 'the lovers' and all that spring he was our friend and he held us together through a fight or two. Summer came and Dana went away for a few months and when she returned it was not the same and we were all very distressed. She tried and I tried and Tiger told us how dumb we were apart, how united together, but it went to hell anyway.

Dana was from the South of the United States and she was all southern, all white. When she kissed Tiger good night at 5 a.m. as we left the bar for home some sins of the past were forgiven, coated in honey and toasted in wine. Tiger laughed because he knew, as perhaps only an ex-name boxer turned garbage collector could, about sin and forgiveness and about love.

In my skiing scrapbooks is a newspaper clipping:

ARMY SKIING STAR CLOCKED AT 109 MPH
Portillo, Los Andes
Chile, Sept. 2 (AP)
Ralph Miller, former Dartmouth skiing star, now serving in the United States Army, today sped down a specially measured 45-degree Andean slope

at a speed of 175.6 kilometers (109 mph) per hour.

He exceeded by 19 kph (12 mph) the former record skiing speed of 156 kph set by Italy's Zeno Colo.

Others who bettered the Colo mark but failed to equal Miller's were Bud Werner of the University of Denver; Marvin Melville of Salt Lake City, Utah; Ronald Funk of Sun Valley, Idaho; and Chick Igaya, the Japanese skier who is attending Dartmouth. All are training for next year's winter Olympic games.

That was in 1955 and I was 16. My school beer drinking fellowship drove automobiles that fast, but the 16 year old mind stampeded at the concept of 109 mph on skis. It magnified the living legends that were Ralph Miller and Bud Werner in the mind of a young ski racer for whom ski racing was everything. The teen age competitor tended to view living people in mythological terms, suspecting that good downhill racers were better humans than poor ones. At the time all downhills frightened me, and I progressed in admiration and sometimes awe of the mythic downhill racer. I studied this breed, reaching to understand what enabled them to go straight where I couldn't or wouldn't. I even categorized courage according to three men—Ralph Miller, Bud Werner and Dick Buek, on anybody's list of the best downhillers of the time.

Ralph Miller's courage was studied, thought out and calculating. Miller looked at possibilities and consequences, prepared better than anyone else and jumped in to do his best. It is revealing that Miller gave up racing to become a doctor. He would have made a great general.

Bud Werner had courage as hard as marble and as cold. Bud gave you chills because once he had chosen his territory there would be no retreat. Bud's courage was win or lose, succeed or die, black or white. Werner said, "When you're afraid of speed it's time to quit." He also said, "There are only two places in a race, first and last." And he must have known some lonely moments. Bud Werner was the leader of an age in American skiing, a peculiar sort of genius, a loner, the last of an American species, and he was loved the most.

Buek possessed a courage opposite to Werner's—hot, loud, indulged in for its own sake. Dick got his kicks more from the moment lived in heat than from the results of the race, though he was a hard, conscientious competitor. Dick was nicknamed "Mad Dog" and he laughed the most. Dick carried the reputation of amazing feats and he enjoyed his life and himself, and he was long dead in a plane wreck before I knew the joy of mastering fear.

Courage was a calculating risk, a primitive hardness or a touch of insanity. What chance had a boy who lacked an essential trait of the brave? I couldn't know then that confidence and resolution are organic and that there are more than three varieties. Each person carries his and her own courage within, and we cease growing when traveling heavy or feeding lean. Like anyone who reflects the past as a future hint I know much now I didn't know then, but I knew there must be a way to true desires and false ones will sooner or later show their hands. I knew a person's endeavors are closely related to their inner needs, and I needed a lot.

In March 1957 something happened in an Aspen bar that followed me around for years.

It was the night of the Roche Cup banquet after the races, the end of a good time. After my first semester of college I moved to Aspen to train and race, living in a rented room with Tony Perry and Ron Funk. Ron was just divorced and leading an athletic, monastic existence and we did not learn to be good friends that year. Tony and I were American college fraternity boys (he an SAE at Denver University and me a Sigma Nu at the University of Nevada, majoring in journalism), and we made up in Aspen social circles for Ron's seclusion. In terms of ski racing it was a discouraging winter, but my 18 year old fraternity house mind saw a form of success (a word one distrusts more each day) in parties, romance, lust and participation in the races. I was sorry the season was over.

I was having a beer in my favorite saloon with my old friend Howie Norton of Piedmont, California. Howie is about 5"6' and 120 pounds. Suddenly, a gentleman estimated at 6'2' and 200 pounds became pushy about ordering a beer and he and Howie exchanged words. Howie was raised in a society where barroom fighting is looked upon the way Norman Mailer must have appeared to Jacqueline Kennedy when he informed her he wanted to write a book proving the Marquis de Sade's sainthood. Howie would no more consider a barroom brawl than he would have invited Lenny Bruce to dinner.

My background did not preclude barroom fighting, but I was clearly outsized and under motivated and told the heavyweight we didn't want any trouble. He asked me if we were 'chicken shit' to fight and I said 'yes' and that seemed to satisfy him and he left, my pride a foolish sacrifice to peace.

Soon, he returned. We learned later that this fighter was a miner, married to the sister of a friend who was one of the best American skiers. He was neither satisfied nor about to be for less than the traditional Saturday night liturgy of a certain strain of man who earns his subsistence by hard, physical labor. Again, he and Howie exchanged words. A disaster was imminent. I got off my stool.

"Hey, man, we don't want any trouble."

He shoved me violently against the bar, hissing obscenities. Next to my right hand on the bar was a full, long-neck bottle of beer. I picked it up. He threw his right which I blocked with my left and I hit him in the head with the bottle of beer. His eyes were like an electric light that has had the current switched off, and when I hit him with the left that had blocked his right it was like knocking over a wooden statue.

End of fight.

The bottle breaking against his head sounded like an explosion. There was blood and excited people. The wounded warrior had a serious concussion and several stitches in his face and head and he spent a few days in the hospital.

The bartender saw it all and he gave me another beer. When the scene quieted I sought out the warrior's wife to apologize and explain my side. Considering her husband's condition, she was quite nice. She wished I hadn't hit him with a bottle but explained with a wife's patience that he had chosen that path before.

Then I sought out the owner of the bar. I'll call this man Number

Seven, a well-known personality, wit, skier and saloon keeper. I apologized. He accepted. In the ensuing years we saw each other many times in the skiing world and always spoke and were friendly.

That night Howie and I left Aspen. A good winter and time in our lives left with us, the fight a good war story, an ugly memory.

At this point let us more closely examine the 1955 AP (Associated Press) story about speed skiing.

Zeno Colo's old record was 159.292 kph, not 156 kph, and neither Werner, Funk, Melville or Igaya bettered that mark. Melville and Igaya were never close, having quit many kilometers slower. The day before Miller's record run Miller and Werner went 158 kph. Funk was clocked at 156 kph but fell in the transition and suffered a badly broken ankle and leg. Ron's fall helped Werner decide that new territory might not be worth the price of holding.

Miller, who had MacArthurian traits, repaired the track after Ron's fall and the next day went up alone as high as possible. Then he came down. He was timed by the great French skier Emile Allais with a hand held stop watch over 50 meters, and his speed was actually measured at 108.7 mph/175.402 kph, not 109 mph. At 100 mph a tenth of a second difference over 50 meters is about 18 mph, and anyone who has ever used a hand stop watch knows that two timers timing the same thing will always have a tenth of a second or more difference. For that reason Miller's run is considered unofficial. He may have only gone 99 mph, but it is just as likely he went 112 mph. People who have raced on the Portillo track and know where he started tend to believe Miller was the first to go over 100 mph.

This revision of the 1955 AP story took me years to learn, and I was interested and spent many hours talking with Ron and others about it. What sort of truth and awareness could exist in the mind of a person who had, for instance, only that newspaper clipping to go on? So much of what we think—therefore do, therefore are—is based on newspaper and television reporting. We of modern civilization and culture are to some extent journalism products. I even majored in journalism in college before switching my major to English and graduating with a journalism minor. One of the better descriptions of journalism was given the world by James Agee:

"Who, what, where, when and why (or how) is the primal cliché and complacency of journalism, but I do not wish to appear to speak favorably of journalism. I have never yet seen a piece of journalism which conveyed more than the slightest fraction of what even moderately reflective and sensitive person would mean and intend by those unachievable words, and that fraction itself I have never seen clean of one or another degree of patent, to say nothing of essential falsehood. Journalism is true in the sense that everything is true to the state of being and to what conditioned and produced it (which is also, but less so perhaps, a limitation of art and science); but that is about as far as its value goes. This is not to accuse or despise journalism for anything beyond its own complacent delusion, that it is telling the truth even of what it tells of. Journalism can within its own limits be 'good' or 'bad,' 'true' or 'false,' but it is not in the nature of journalism even to approach any less relative degree of truth. Again, journalism is not to be blamed for this; no more than a cow is to be blamed for not being a horse. The difference is, and the reason one can respect or anyhow approve of the cow, that few cows can have the delusion or even the desire to be horses, and that none of them could get away with it even with a small part of the public. The very blood and semen of journalism, on the contrary, is a broad and successful form of lying. Remove that form of lying and you no longer have journalism."

Part of the answer to why a man finds himself in big speed on a pair of skis is involved in and attributed to the journalistic mind. The American of my age was reared as much by journalistic media as by family and school, and I do not think it has changed. There is something uncomfortable about the desire to be better than other people, but the newspapers said it was a good way to be, and to a sports oriented teenager the path lay through the self-conscious swamp of his own fear, lack of knowledge and unripe skill. Step by step.

This is a methodical approach to one-upmanship, as opposed to more spontaneous forms of the game, but evolution is in evidence here. By continuing through the swamp of fear (or any other swamp), familiarity will make the difficulty known, then understood, then natural and bearable. By persevering through eternally new swamps of the mind man has progressed to his present state. By forgetting where he came from while never letting go of what he came through man binds his vision and freedom and lives on the brink of a threatening tomorrow, neglecting the fullness that is today. I learned something about this through speed skiing.

And then there was Bob Beattie. In 1961 he became the first full time U.S. Ski Team coach, in no small part because of Bud Werner's support. Werner had faith that Bob was the man to bring the American ski racing program up to the level of the European programs. Or better them. In 1961 that was a monumental task. As it turned out Bud's faith was justified, as faith often is, but Beattie had a great deal to learn and he trod upon legions of unwary toes during his education. Bob brought organization, order and politics on a grand scale into American ski racing. Some of us viewed ski racing as free expression and we resented, defied and scorned organization, politics and enforced order. And there was conflict. And toes stomped upon. And Beattie had very big feet.

CHAPTER TWO

"The world is always burning, burning with the fire of greed, anger and ignorance; one should flee from such danger as soon as possible."

Buddha

THE WINTER OF 1961-62 was a good year of competitive skiing for me. A comeback year. I had been out of racing for two years with a broken leg entailing some surgeries and other personal disasters. Those were my dark ages.

Several times during that period Ron Funk proved himself helpful, encouraging, interested—a friend—at the proper time. Timing is important in friendship and other things. In the late summer of 1960, after I had been living in unhappy circumstances in Palo Alto, California, I left and went to Lake Tahoe and the mountains that I love. My ride let me out along the highway near South Shore with a suitcase of clothes, a typewriter, less than $100 and no plan. I was relieved to be out of Palo Alto and back in the mountains but only vaguely aware of what the next move might be. At that moment Ron Funk walked out of the woods.

A coincidence beyond awareness.

"Hey, Man, what're you doing?" he asked.

Within an hour I had a comrade, a place to stay and a job.

Another time, autumn 1961, I was living in Berkeley, attending classes at the University of California, sporting a huge mustache, finished with skiing

(I told myself and anyone who would listen), dieting on beer and spaghetti, seeping myself in the complete letters of Van Gogh in the Kroeber Library, and limping badly when the weather was cold or the draft board hot. Funk had just returned from making a movie with Dick Barrymore in New Zealand. He heard I was in the neighborhood and tracked me down, and I was hard to find in those days. I showed Ron my Berkeley existence and he told me about his summer in New Zealand, Australia, Tokyo, Saigon, Hong Kong and Honolulu.

Funk has had more injuries than you would think one man's karma could accrue, but he was still racing, traveling, doing what he wanted and still seeking. After talking with him I looked more closely at what I had been allowing a broken leg and a few disasters to do to my life. Most of the world had it much worse. I was feeling sorry for myself, a shameful trait. Funk, then, friend and comrade, was also a personal example.

A couple of months later as I was leaving a night class I saw a poster announcing a Sverre Engen ski movie on campus. I dropped in and was stunned to see on film the fall which had broken my leg and ankle. It was surreal to be as I was, where I was, doing what I was doing with and to myself, and to see movies of skiing and mountains and snow and old friends and other, better, times. That was all I needed. After the movie I caught a midnight bus to Reno. Within six weeks I lost 21 pounds, enrolled once more at the University of Nevada, worked out in the gym and forced my ever-decreasing bulk around some 10,000 slalom poles.

In February 1962 I won my first ski race in three years, the Silver Dollar Derby and Far West Championships, placing first in the slalom and second (to Funk) in the downhill. Afterwards, we were celebrating, singing, telling jokes and flirting with the girls when Ron called for a toast: "Here's to you, Dick, and the restoration of a badly abused ego."

Funk understood, and I was very much warmed, strengthened and motivated by that understanding.

That season exceeded all skiing expectations. It was desperately difficult to get a fair start seeding (starting order groups which in theory give the best racers the earlier starting positions and thereby the better and faster course conditions) outside the Far West, but such things were usual by

1962 for what I called the 'free expressionists' of skiing. However, in the spring I was named to the All-American Ski Team and in the fall to the first U.S. National Training team.

The Olympic tryouts were the following winter and I spared no pains in preparation. By autumn I was in the best physical and mental conditioning for ski racing I had known. The relationship with Dana had dissolved and I was in my final semester of college. Life revolved around school, work, working out and preparing for the tryouts.

From my journal, October 14, 1962:

School and work and working out has made it impossible to write here as I should like. School is good on some counts, bad on others. ROTC (the only course I ever failed and was forced to retake) is not too bad, but simply a complete and ridiculous waste of time.

My training is very good. I'm in the best shape of my life...I feel as if something has changed in me in the last few months. We will wait and see, but I don't think I'm the same person I was two months ago.

...meanwhile, I'm an emotional hermit, which suits me as it doesn't bother or hurt anyone, including myself...Right now you are an emotional hermit and a hell of a skier. You are trying to be less emotional, more of a hermit, and a hell of a lot better a hell of a skier. Got that? I hope so.

It has snowed and I skied all day with my fine friend Mike Brunetto. The first day is not really skiing, but it was tremendous to be in the sun and snow and in the mountains.

Life is really a thesaurus and everyone wants it to stop at being a dictionary.

In December the first USSA Vail training camp was held. A pattern for the year was established. Jim Gaddis, the preceding year's National Giant Slalom and NCAA slalom champion, myself and several others were put in a group coached by a man whose personal skiing technique peaked at the advanced stem and whose knowledge was a step behind his abilities. Gaddis and I asked Willy Schaeffler if we could join his group and he said we could and agreed with our reasons for doing so. A day later

Beattie told us we would ski with the first coach or leave the camp. That's how it had been organized and that's how it would be done and Bob was not up for discussing the matter. Jim and I skied with the incompetent (obviously there to satisfy some political faction of the USSA). We helped each other while politely listening to the coach who was a nice person but hopelessly inept as a ski mentor. Jim and I began to deal with the dawning awareness that our Olympic aspirations were not encouraged or, even, welcome.

The camp ended with two races. I was placed in the last seed in both races and did not belong there and said so to Beattie. Seedings that year became an insult against which one had no recourse. Like many people, anger is one of my reactions to disappointment. Anger shreds concentration and destroys happiness and satisfaction with the present moment, and it has never helped anyone accomplish anything constructive.

Patterns.

Journal, January 6, 1963:

One must have infinite patience and steel strong discipline when one is trying as hard as he knows how and not succeeding and, more, failing. Otherwise you are given up to despair. My skiing is not what it should be and I do not know what else there is to do about it. All I can do is have patience and not panic. I have raced three times...and I have been very poor in each race. I have faith or I could not maintain patience or discipline, but it hurts inside the discipline and fortification to perform this way.

Two weeks later I graduated from the University of Nevada. Ten hours after my last examination Mike Brunetto and I were in Sun Valley for the Sun Valley Open Championships.

We were too late for the giant slalom and could only race the slalom. I ran in the last seed, dead last one run, and finished 5th. The starting position made me angry and my finish assured me that sort of thing couldn't continue. In the next few months I learned something of the difference between assurance and presumption.

We were scheduled to leave the next day for Colorado and the next weekend's Broadmoor slalom derby, the first Olympic tryout race. Slalom was my best event at the time and I was eager, prepared, ready to perform.

That night Funk asked if I wanted to try for a Diamond Sun. I said "sure," though I wasn't. The Diamond Sun may be the most difficult standard race in the world. It is the fastest I know of and starts on top of Bald Mountain and finishes at the Wood River, 2 3/5 miles below. The route is any way possible down Ridge, Rock Garden, Canyon and River Run. It had been run only twice since World War II, but the mountain was almost perfect for it and Funk loved speed. Winning a Diamond sun would be a fitting conclusion to racing for a man who was happiest going fast on a pair of skis.

We spent two wonderful days practicing. It was my first taste of extreme speed. The only thing in my mind, aside from the pragmatic problems of the course, was the ambition to have a Diamond Sun. Not many men had them.

The snow was about a foot deep, smooth and ice hard. Rock Garden was imperfectly covered, so we were forced to a low, left line very close to the trees. This made the turn into Canyon very difficult and put us ten feet of fall-away ice from trees at high speed all the way down Rock Garden, but it was all we could do.

Jack Reddish, the best American ski racer of the late 1940s and early '50s, was vacationing in the Valley and gave me very helpful advice. He showed me a line off the road at the top of canyon that I had not seen. He also said not to practice the big, fast schusses in a course more than once. If you were in shape for the bumps and turns the really high speeds should be saved for the race, the implication being that survival in big speeds was as much a matter of chance than skill. I have learned to disagree with this kind of thinking. Jack was speaking of the Canyon schuss, which I estimated at 80 mph at the bottom, but I remembered his words some months later.

Journal, January 27, 1963:

On a train between Provo, Utah and Glenwood Springs, Colorado, on the way to Aspen.

I won the Diamond Sun on the 23rd, setting a new record of 2:21:4. I averaged about 65 mph and must have reached 80 coming out of Canyon. Since downhill runners are born, not made, and I am not a born downhiller, it was a testimony to my self-control. I was very pleased and proud and, at the same time, humble. Never have I reached or achieved higher in skiing.

Funk probably would have beaten me, but he fell. I honestly would have gladly given up the record to him. It meant more to him, and he is the kind of friend you do not begrudge having what he wants, even at your expense. (Funk, despite a fall, had a time of 2:31, earning a Diamond Sun.)

Tammy Dix also won a Sun in 2:36. That time will stand for the women for a long time.

....It is apparent that I am not being encouraged by the powers in my Olympic bid. Well....fuck Beattie and his favorites and the others. I feel very confident.

The day after the Diamond Sun I phoned the Broadmoor. Beattie told me an entry would be sent and it had not showed up. I was hungry after the 5th in slalom starting at the end of the field and the Diamond Sun. Number Seven by then was out of his saloon and into the Broadmoor and I got him on the phone. He told me with a flack man's glad hand sincerity that he was extremely sorry, but my name had not been turned in to the Broadmoor by the USSA. He was even more sorry that entries were closed. No, there was no way. There must have been a mix-up somewhere, but it wasn't Number Seven's fault. He was very sorry and said he'd see me over in Colorado next time I was there and hung up.

I was frustrated and furious and I knew not at whom, though Beattie was obvious. I was a member of the national training team, had been elected to the previous year's All-American Ski Team, was among the better slalom skiers in the country, had spent six months preparing myself as hard and as well as I knew how, and I had just done the best skiing of my life. I was so ready I could taste it.

And I couldn't get into the first race.

The cliché is that it all comes out in the wash. A few days before I arrived in Aspen it all came out of Number Seven. Some of it, anyway. One early morning after Seven had been salooning for several hours in the Aspen watering holes my name came up in conversation. My friend Don McKinnen was with the group and mentioned that it was a shame I hadn't been allowed to race at Broadmoor as I seemed to be skiing well.

McKinnen reported to me that Seven grew very angry and said something to the effect, "So long as I have anything to say about it, Dorworth won't get into any race. Anyone who would try to gouge out a man's eyes with a beer bottle shouldn't be allowed to race." He went on to malign my character, motivations and mind with stories of the fight of '57, which happened, and manifestations of his mind which did not. But that was the essence of it.

Hard at the time to believe an adult man could feel that way (impossible to know his thinking) six years after an 18 year old boy was involved in a brawl in his saloon. Especially since he had always been cordial to my face every time we met in the intervening years.

Funk said, "Those Colorado boys stick close together."

My own feelings were strong and I fought with anger and they were mixed with thoughts of crystal clarity. After a series of poor performances in the Colorado races I returned to Sun Valley to earn my winter as a busboy in the Challenger Inn.

Journal, February 22, 1963:

It is Washington's birthday. On this symbolic occasion of freedom it should be put here that I am free, happy, and looking forward—always forward—to a better life. Though I could not make the Olympic team if I won every remaining tryout, skiing has been fine to me and I will not desert it. I am more free on skis than anywhere else. No one is ever free from anything, but it makes me feel good to think so, and, so, I will think so.

Journal, February 28, 1963:

Today I sent a letter to Number Seven, a copy to Bob Beattie. The letter will do no good—especially for me—but one must voice his disapproval of the shits every now and then. It is sad that the shits control skiing. It is the same everywhere.

Another letter went to Howard Head. I turned down his job offer. It would have been good and it would have been secure and I would have been respectable. But such things are not for me.

I have not made myself more popular to the world in the last 24 hours.

I am getting pretty detached from what the world thinks of me. Most of the world is made up of shits, so it doesn't matter what they think. All that really matters are the things that make you feel good. Fine friends, skiing, making love, brandy and good music make one feel good. Those things matter.

The letter to Seven, copy to Beattie, read:

Number:

I had hoped to run into you while I was in Colorado so that I could speak with you rather than write a letter. Letters are incomplete.

My personal feelings about your keeping me out of the Broadmoor Slalom Derby are not important, but I was extremely surprised to learn that you would do such a thing because of something that happened when I was 18 years old. I had thought you a bigger and better man, and a more intelligent one.

There are, however, two things which are important in your actions. The first is that you have kept a competitor out of an Olympic tryout race simply because of your personal prejudices. If you (the Broadmoor) are good enough to put on a tryout race, then you should choose your racers according to their Olympic aspirations and potential rather than by one man's judgment of their personality and values. It is not your place or right to say who is eligible to enter an Olympic tryout race. That you have exercised the influence and power you have in this manner does not speak well of you, or of the Broadmoor Slalom Derby. That you have been allowed to does not speak well of Bob Beattie or the United States Olympic movement.

The second thing which is important is that you are at least partly wrong in your stated reasons for banning me from races which you are connected with. You made a statement to at least one person to the effect that "Anyone who tries to gouge the eyes out of a man with a broken bottle and pulls seats out from under pregnant women will never get in any race I'm connected with." You were speaking of me in defense of keeping me out of the Broadmoor race. So far as the pregnant lady goes, I don't know what you're talking about. You are mistaken or ad-libbing or some such thing. In March 1957 I hit a man with a beer bottle in your saloon. The man I hit started the fight, forced it, and allowed me no way out. There are witnesses to this. I explained this to you (in word and letter) at the time. Apparently that, and my apology, were not enough. While I do not excuse myself for hitting a man with a bottle, there is a considerable difference between that and "trying to gouge the eyes out of a man with a broken bottle."

I resent your mistaken exaggeration of past events which concern me as much as I am surprised by them. I am disappointed that I was kept from an important Olympic tryout race, and a race important to later seedings. I was saddened to see evidence that one person's prejudice and dislike of a competitor (no matter how righteous you may feel, it is, after all, only personal prejudice) can keep that competitor from racing. I, and others, had better hopes of the "new drive and goal" in United States skiing.

While I expect nothing in the way of general or specific betterment in yourself or anyone else because of this letter, I felt it should be written...... and read.

Dick Dorworth

All life is intertwined like the strands of a rug, forms and relationships determined by color.

. . . .

I resolved to stay in Sun Valley, train and give everything in the Harriman Cup and the National Championships in Alaska. My plans, unencumbered by organization or expectation, progressed freely and well. Then, on March 6, three weeks before the Harriman, I was hospitalized with mumps, an uncommon, unfunny, child's infection for a 24 year old. I knew nothing of karma in those days, but I was learning.

A few days later Funk broke his ankle in downhill practice in Solitude, Utah.

After eight days I was out of the hospital. The year was not finished nor was my store of resolution, but the stream was not going my way. My skiing picked up remarkably fast. All those months of training paid me back.

Journal, March 28, 1963:

The night before the Harriman downhill. I have practiced for three days and done well...Today was the non-stop...I feel confident of success. Beattie did his best against me and that is quite a lot. He seeded me so low that only three men...run after I do.

I think it was the great French skier Perillat who said, "You must not think too much" and "Your must not let your imagination become an obsession."

Perillat referred to the fears of downhill, but any course can be viewed as a microcosm of a man's life.

Whatever was my part as an American racer in the United States racing scene, it ended with the seeding for the Harriman downhill. So did the last naïve belief. I felt somewhat the way I imagine a young, puritan, he-man type must when he discovers his favorite sister sleeps with the neighborhood hippie. That feeling went with me to Chile.

One thing happened during the Harriman races which still makes me smile. I was waiting my turn near the slalom start. It was the day after the downhill in which my finish was some forty places higher than my start, and I had another Siberian seed for the slalom. Beattie was milling around with his boys. I avoided him, demurring to spill out the unpleasantness I felt. I was so angry my mind was only secondarily concerned with slalom.

Bob suddenly walked up to me, put his arm around me father-like, and said, "Hey, buddy, that was a fine downhill you ran yesterday."

Like a handhold breaking off during a difficult climbing move, a handhold of the mind. "Now wait a minute, Bob," I said, "don't fuck me and pat me on the back too. That's too much."

Most of the ensuing conversation I don't remember now. It wasn't pleasant. Bob said I'd have been better off not writing the letter to Seven and that he (Beattie) would never screw me. What I wish I had pointed out to Bob but didn't is that I was far better off having written the letter than I would have been keeping silent, and when I pointed out that it was too late, that he already had screwed me, Beattie showed his best Vermont marble smile and said that things would get better.

Since that moment Bob has been as good as his word. To me, anyway. I had a good seeding for the next day's giant slalom (and a better result), and while I was left out of the next year's national training camps the remainder of my seedings were fair if too late to be of use.

The night of the Harriman Cup banquet I was awarded the Jimmy Griffith Award for sportsmanship and outstanding contribution to the sport of skiing. This was a big honor and I was and am proud to share the award with Funk, Buek, Reddish, Phil Puchner, Monty Skinner and Jack Simpson. I wasn't aware the award was going to be given, and when it was Jack Simpson made a nice speech in my honor and applause resounded through the Sun Valley Lodge dining room. There are, after all, free expressionists left in skiing. At least, appreciationists.

But I wasn't there.

After the races, seedings and other events I felt so little a part of the Harriman Cup and the racing scene that I missed the banquet, spending the evening drinking beer in Slavey's with a favorite friend. One of the attractions of the saloon for the disenchanted is that so long as you pay your quarter you will receive your glass of beer, a simple transaction in a common institution, its own commonness saving its honesty.

. . . .

From Sun Valley we went to Anchorage, Alaska for the U.S. National Championships. The season's goal was abandoned. My notebooks show observations about the countryside and thoughts of people and little concern with ski racing. I raced for the pure joy of the race, without a care for the finish. I had my best result of a disastrous season, a 7th in the giant slalom.

After the races we flew to Seattle where Funk met us. Ron and I were headed back to off season Sun Valley and Jim Gaddis and Art Brookstrom rode with us as far as Boise.

During the long drive we talked about the year. Gaddis had not received much encouragement toward making the Olympic team, but he had had an excellent season. By any objective standards Jim was clearly on the team. I told him what a great thing he had accomplished—beating a hostile system at its own game—but Jim said he was sure his name would be left off the team. I thought and said that it was impossible to pick an Olympic team that year without Gaddis.

The objective thinker is slow to learn because he has a hard time believing some people are the way they are. He can't accept the reason and therefore ignores the fact.

Marcelle Barkley Herz was my maternal aunt. She was one of those rare people who make the world a better place just by their presence. The first year I skied she was the Nevada State Champion in slalom and downhill. How fine it was to be 11 years old and the nephew of the champion of Nevada.

Marcelle ski bummed in Sun Valley in the '30s and was a fine athlete in several sports. She was a teacher, a person who gives. Sometimes she had a school in which to teach, often her own, less frequently public, and she always led by personal example. She was responsible for the inception of Reno's Junior Ski Program which today takes over 2500 children skiing every weekend.

I was the only one in the family seriously involved in skiing and 'Marcie' was always enthused about and aware of what I was doing and how it was going. She made a point of giving encouragement in hard times. Simple things like encouragement were rare for me I sometimes thought, and they were appreciated. So was Marcelle Herz.

CHAPTER THREE

The lost end of the rainbow

SOME OF THE PRECEDING may read like sour grapes about a time and team long past and a personal dislike for the spoilers of the wine. This is so only to the extent that bitterness was part of my state of mind before going to Chile and during the events that unfolded there. More important was the hard (and hard earned) knowledge of something not right. (Note: It took a few years but Beattie and I mended fences and became friends, and I have come to very much admire and respect him as a man and for his many contributions to skiing and to many skiers. And, to show how far life can evolve with good intention and some effort, I value his friendship and understand and even respect what he did concerning me and some others without agreeing with it. Number Seven, however, sank even lower in my view. Many years later I was Director of the Aspen Mountain Ski School, a position with a certain cachet in the ski world, and every time we met Seven treated me to a huge, insincere smile, a glad hand and a surface chatter for the sake of whoever was around implying we were the best of old friends, comrades in cachet. I added phony to my list of his character infirmities.)

And there is this: Had I been given the opportunities I felt I deserved in that Olympic tryout year and been fortunate enough to have been named to the team, I would never have entered the world of speed skiing which taught and gave me so much. Without becoming metaphysical or woo woo, life really does have its own reasons. I also came to realize how immaturity and a psychological instability destroyed much of my effectiveness as a racer, not to mention the other things of life. Personal problems can ruin a racer if he lets them, but those same hang ups may push him through his doubts to inner honesty. I had weaknesses I wouldn't or couldn't recognize. I also had strength, but it is obvious that a man with peace in his mind and love in his heart has no need for world records. This is only to explain a bit of why I did.

Feeling neglected by my way of life I sought to show more, give more and—the ancient folly—to prove myself. My task was to show "them." I forgot to remember that when people are with you a little is enough, and when they are not everything is not.

And I was of a different time, an older rhythm than the one that came in on Beattie's cadence. The first year I went to Sun Valley Stein Eriksen, Christian Pravda, Dick Buek, Jack Reddish, Dean Perkins, Otto Von Allman, Hans Nogler Herbert Jochum and several other less gifted racers were living, working and training there. That was 1953, the year the fastest, most dangerous Harriman Cup downhill was run in a blizzard at the cost of several broken legs, at least one broken back and the job of the course setter. Watching people like that ski made a potent impression on my 14 year old mind. Each of those fine skiers had to earn his way along with skiing. That was acceptable, the way it was. A boy's dream was to be good enough in racing to one day work, live and ski with the likes of Pravda, Buek, Reddish and the others. To be better than they seemed impossible, for who in 1953 could hope to ski like Stein?

By 1963 I was likely the best racer in Sun Valley except Christian who was seldom there. Times had changed and the best U.S. racers no longer lived as semi-bums in Ketchum, Aspen or Stowe. Most of them went to school and their lives revolved around a national program instead of around the palpitations of ski resort existence. The era of the lone racer was over. Its difficult and unsteady passing was a necessary step that had to be made before another could be. It is ironic that the first force behind this change was Bud Werner, the pioneer, the loner, the great ski racer who broke the way and who did not retreat. Bud recognized the need and logic of a new way before anyone else and he helped usher in Beattie to fill the need because no one else could. But there were some who understood the logic without being able to fit the mold and remain themselves, and the latter is important.

I was, then, strung between two stages of American ski racing, one dead and the other just being born. While I was not quite dead neither was I just born. Part of what happened in Chile was making my place in my sport, in my own way, in my own good time.

. . . .

Early in the 1962-63 season Ron Funk began talking about a speed run. He had tried it in 1955 and fell at more than 90 mph and badly broke his ankle. The injury hampered his racing career and he became well known for the fastest fall in skiing history. There are professional purple heart personalities who derive perverse satisfaction from such reputation, but Funk is of a different tribe. When the game is to succeed it is a constant irritant to be recognized and defined by one horrendous fall. That's part of it, though only Ron could explain his motivations, but it's fair to say that the long game of ski racing was about over and everyone wants the big one that got away. Also, there are the deep drives (hereditary? psychological? psychotic? neurotic?) more evident in Funk than most.

Ron asked me to go with him. I said I would but there were several problems, the first being that I am no daredevil. Despite the desire to indulge in the great folly, Quixotic assaults on my reality are not part of my nature. I was 24 years old, a recent college graduate, and about out of acceptable (to those who give and withhold acceptance) reasons for not going to work and blasting my hole in society. I had valid uses for gainful employment, including a forcibly patient ex-wife who had legal claim to a great deal of money I never had or ever would. I didn't know if I should continue racing, to pursue the path I'd been following or to give in to the tide I'd fought so long. Should I assume a respectability of Kennedy-like enthusiasm or hold the line, risking emulation of the angry old man, the universal eccentric? Good questions consciously contemplated.

If the inner questions were resolved in favor of Chile, there remained the practical problems of getting there, living, training and, I hoped, returning.

Further complications existed because Howard Head who founded and owned Head Ski Company had offered me a good job. Such employment answers many questions for a young man, though it was clear then and crystal clear now that a company job is not necessarily the best thing a man can do with the time of his short life.

As the season thrashed on and I wrestled with the present, future and, in the case of Number Seven, the past, I came to one conclusion: whatever had caused me to race all those years was not yet understood, completed, resolved. The decision and the understanding had nothing to do with success or failure, making teams or avoiding work. One must heed the inner winds the way gliders ride the air currents. Whatever the price, whoever else I might become, I would not allow myself to become the middle-age or senior ski racer who didn't take care of it in the proper place and rhythm of life, the ski racing equivalent of the frustrated ex-football player who picks Saturday night bar fights as his contribution to that afternoon's game.

The job was declined with thanks and the honest explanation that I had other things to do that were more important to me. I would continue to race.

The next decision was a commitment to go with Ron, to run for pure speed. As an organism cannot be dissected without destroying it one reason for a decision cannot be isolated and set aside. In nature everything is connected and continually evolving in all directions. If the reader cannot find here all the links to the decisions I made he should look to his own creative experiences and acts. The connections are all there. The important thing to see and grasp is commitment, spoken, final, irreversible commitment to try one's best.

Funk began writing, planning, phoning, talking, seeking financial backing. That was frustrating and discouraging. Dozens of communications with magazines, newspapers, manufacturers, ski clubs and wealthy prospective patrons of the sporting arts and the great folly paid off with two backers—Head Ski Company for the advertising potential and Ski Magazine for the story, whatever it turned out to be. (See Ski Magazine, February, March 1964)

The final issue for me was resolved by Tony Racloz, a French ski instructor in Sun Valley, unlikely enough in Austrian dominated Sun Valley. Tony was the ski school director in La Parva, Chile, and he offered me a job including round trip transportation and time off for big speed.

It was settled except for the organization and action. Organization was mostly paper work, talk, running around, talk, waiting, talk and talk. We will pass most of that by.

. . . .

In late May Racloz and I left Los Angeles by drive-away car for New Orleans to catch the Italian freighter Giorgio Parodi which would take us to Chile. Frenchman was a perfect traveling companion with his wide smile, bon vivant mentality and a wide range of living and traveling experience in Europe, Africa, South America, Canada and the United States. The captain and crew of the Giorgio Parodi were hospitable and engaging hosts at sea. The trip across America, my first view of New Orleans, the boat ride down the Mississippi, in the Gulf and past Cuba, through the Panama Canal and down the west coast of South America are some of my best traveling memories. Notes of this period cover observations, feelings and experiences. There is no mention of the speed run and few thoughts about skiing.

Journal May 30, 1963:

I saw a rainbow this afternoon while I was exercising on the deck. But I could only see one end of it where it rose from the water and disappeared into clouds. I could not for the life of me find the other end of the rainbow. It bothered me because I have never before seen only half a rainbow. I searched the horizon and scanned the clouds, and still I could not find the other end. I did not like it that way and between exercises when I was resting I kept on looking. And, finally, I looked to where I thought it should have been and it was there, apparent and beautiful. I wondered if it had been there all the time and I had missed it or if it had only become visible because I looked so hard. I was delighted to find it, and when I looked back to the first end to link them together in a continuity it was gone. I could find it nowhere and I had no doubt that it was gone forever.

How like life is this little experience. If you see the beginning of a rainbow (or one end, for who knows which is the beginning and which the end?) and care enough to follow it through and find the other end, then, when you get there in all your happiness and success and you are extremely fortunate if you have either, you cannot find the end from which you started. The beginning is gone forever. You may have success and happiness but you do not know why, you are empty inside for lack of the lost end of the rainbow.

How like life!

If you do not seek the other end of the rainbow you still have the one you first saw. Perhaps you are not so empty but certainly you are never fulfilled.

How like life!

The truly unfortunate is the one who sees one end of the rainbow and strikes out after the other and never finds it and who has then lost, forever, the first end.

Everybody sees rainbows, I know, but he would be a fortunate man who never saw any. But he would be a dull man.

How like life!

I wonder is there is any man who has both ends of the rainbow? If there is such a man I could show you contentment.

A June 5 list of my daily exercises shows that something besides rainbows was on my mind:

40 push ups

40 sit ups

80 leg wheels

10 hand together push ups

10 hand pointed out push ups

50 leg raises

400 quick knee bends in egg position

8 underarm pull ups

40 leg raise swivels

5 complete sets of stretching exercises

6 overarm pull ups

40 sit ups

60 leg wheels

35 push ups

40 leg raises

A further indication of my state of mind in seen in this comment inspired by the death of Pope John XIII in my journal of June, 5, 1963:

The pope is dead. Now he sees whether everything or anything he said and lived for was true. I would not bet on it but I hope so. What a grotesque joke on the pope if, after all, he is only worm food and nothing more. But it is no more grotesque or cruel than other aspects of the human animal. War and nationalism, for instance.

Not until June 24, several days after arriving in Chile, do my notes mention speed skiing. I had encountered Sergio Navarette and Tito Beladone, two old friends and icons of Chilean skiing, in Santiago. They were very interested in our speed attempt, had the necessary electronic timing equipment and pledged their total support.

That same day a quote from Philip Wylie appears in my journal:

"In spite of the dangers evident in modern forms of war, a revolt from boredom has had much to do with the fact that it is possible to launch these wars. Man was designed by nature to hunt, to struggle, to endure, and to achieve on a personal physical plane; all his glands and hormones are integrated for such dangerous and exciting affairs. It is not normal for the creature to immolate himself for eight or ten hours a day, five or six days a week, in the acrid din of factories, where he is fairly secure but where he does the same one thing forever."

Philip Wylie, 1942

Funk arrived toward the end of June and immediately set to work at Portillo. On July 2 I received word that Gaddis hadn't been named to the Olympic team. My journal of that day reflects:

My very worst fears about the Olympic team are true. That is disillusioning even when you are not naïve about skiing politics. God damn.... and....and....and all their kind. The next time I see Beattie I'll recommend that the next time there be no tryouts and that the politicians simply pick the teams according to their own prejudices. (They would say judgment but that would not be correct.) That way a lot of people would not bother to spend so much of themselves to no end. I do not like what is inside me when I think of this. It is bitter and poisonous and thoughts are not clear when it is there. Outside of Funk and a few others I must be careful what I say when this feeling is in me.

The speed run syndrome began to wind up.

Journal July 4, 1963:

It is good to have Funk in Chile. He understands the best because his interest comes from the spirit and only secondarily from the mind. He is going to Portillo now and will send for me in 3 or 4 weeks. Then I will test my nerve, my resolution, my physical and mental strength—and my ability to hold the lowest crouch at 100 mph. No matter what happens we are attempting the right and honorable thing. For Funk it is an adventure. For me it is an undertaking. For both of us it will be unforgettable.

Within the next month or two it might be possible to focus all that is me and my life into a very few screaming seconds on a big hill at Portillo.

I await thee, Fate, thou fickle, wonderful bitch.

On July 23 I went to Portillo planning to take care of the entire speed run in four days. That's more than a little like Walter Mitty at the wheel.

‘ ‘ ‘ ‘ ‘ ‘

The Portillo speed track inspires awe. Completely devoid of trees or rocks, it appears a nearly vertical wall of snow leading up to overhanging rock cliffs. It is called Ralph Miller's Run after the man who showed the possibilities of the hill and I had not seen it in five years. The train ride up to Portillo from Los Andes was slow, circuitous and beautiful and the size of the Andes alters a man's perspective. I was very excited on the train and thought of Portillo in 1958 and of the people who made that summer—Willy and Rosmarie Bogner, Jim Laird, Rip McManus, Roger Hackley, Roger Crist, Dave Pruett, John Koppes, Phil Potvin, Laurie Gibb, Kalevi Hakkinen, Mal Swenson, Vicho Vera, Victor Tagle,

Jaime Braun, Fernando Karlezi and the flamboyant and incredible Stein
Eriksen who gave his time, knowledge and friendship because he liked
our attempt at racing. I remembered the people and relationships from
that time and I knew what had happened to a lot of them. I thought of
myself in 1958—19 years old, a crew cut college fraternity boy in white
bucks who believed in a life so easy that the only reason people failed is
that they didn't try hard enough. I remembered endless hours of slalom
practice and the discipline of attempt, assured that the reward for push-
ing so hard was just around the corner, continuing to practice on ankles
so sprained that tears came to my eyes once on the hill and letting go so
seldom that when it came it was like the water of a burst dam, nature
repressed. I thought of five years difference in myself, returning to a place
of another time with fewer (or at least different) illusions and dreams. In
those years I had learned that trying hard is only one link, not enough by
itself, and I was impressed (with myself) at how clearly I saw everything
compared to my vision in 1958. There had been a river of living under
the bridge and at 24 I was learning to know myself and, thus, the world.
What I couldn't know was that this learning was completely natural,
normal and would continue as long as life.

I kept to myself during the ride, avoiding the skiers bound for Portillo,
including a southern California beach girl far too pretty to ignore and an amazing British Olympic skier, Richard Salm, who later became a friend. I preferred
my thoughts, starting the long wind up for the big come down. As the train
approached Portillo my excitement grew in expectation of seeing in the perfect
Andean afternoon a well groomed straight track on the face of Ralph Miller's
run. I looked when it came into view. And then I looked again. I could barely
believe or contain my disappointment at what I saw—nothing. There was not a
track on the entire face.

A pattern was established.

Llewellyn Gross was Marcelle's sister. She and her husband built Harvey's Wagon Wheel on the south shore of Lake Tahoe. When I was a
boy Llewellyn was a fine cook and she cooked enough for everyone and
a bit more. Her warm heart showed in her smile. She had the untidy

custom of allowing alcohol to loosen tongue and fist and to call a spade just that and to perform other socially unwise or at least uncomfortable maneuvers.

The Wagon Wheel grew larger and more successful and the Gross' responsibilities, fortunes, problems and wars of mind grew accordingly. Llewellyn grew wiser and less spontaneous, giving more of things and less of herself. This most human of women had supported much of my skiing, including the first year in Aspen and the 1958 trip to Chile, but by 1963 she disapproved of much of my life and while she never withheld her love and we remained very close she would no longer support my path.

Llewellyn and Marcelle were very close in spirit and my two favorites.

Nearer my God to Thee

JOURNAL, JULY 23, 1963:

Pan American Hotel, Santiago. 2 a.m. I leave for Portillo in 6 hours. The next four days may be crucial to my life—or I may be a dramatic sentimentalist. However, I know some things. We will have a go at the speed run, and I am prepared for whatever happens. I am more alive than ever.

Journal, July 23, 1963:

Portillo. Willy Bogner is here. We exchanged greetings and he has grown into a fine looking man. He is having ankle trouble, so we also exchanged medical inquiries. The last time I saw him was at Portillo five years ago. A lot has happened in that time, but he came closer to immortality than I. However, we shall see. The race is not over yet.

We will not seriously run for speed this week but we will do some other things, mostly for the cameras.

At tea this afternoon my old waiter remembered me as "El campeon de Chile" and I remembered him as my old waiter. We both felt pride in being remembered as what we were. There was also satisfaction in remembering. It made me feel very good.

I blush to have written about immortality and the race not being over, but I wrote it and that's important.

The track was not prepared because it had snowed since Ron Sent for me and neither timing nor officials would be continuously available during the next few weeks. We needed both. We had not traveled 6,000 miles to risk everything on an unrecognized record like Miller's. Dick Barrymore was there so we decided to run for cameras and experience. It seemed confused to me and I limited my attention to the mountain, the snow and the pragmatic problems of speed.

By this time C.B. Vaughan of Manchester, Vermont had joined us. C.B., a red-head, freckle-face veteran of the U.S. racing circuit was head of the Portillo Ski Patrol. He was not hyper-motivated and his interest in speed was that of a clean, new game, but we had talked about it the previous winter and C.B. is a hundred percenter in all he does. This quality later showed itself clearly, invaluably.

The first task was to prepare a track. According to the polarized logic of our inexperience we needed a perfect track, "as smooth as a baby's bottom." To become airborne or have a drifting tip at 100 mph is in the realm of possibility where imagination shudders at its own creative potential for destruction. Our goal was unattainable perfection. The harder we tried, the closer we came, the more perfectly groomed was the track, the higher went our standards and the further away our aim. Finally, settling for what we had we got to the task—speed.

There are degrees of danger even in actions which are more dangerous than the ordinary perils of living on our contaminated earth. Ignorance and bad faith weigh down what does not survive. I often look back on my experiences and actions and see the blessings of luck, and I am struck with wonder by my own past ignorance.

Later experiences with big speeds in Italy taught me that in Portillo we were inexpressibly lucky. Our chore was to take a huge white wall of snow against a cliff and prepare with skis, rakes and shovels and not enough people to help a track ten yards wide and a half mile long, all the while convinced that the slightest imperfection in terrain could result in anything from a broken leg to the loss of life itself.

Despite our fanatic concern with the smoothness of the track, at one point there was a five foot wall of snow a few feet right of where we passed through the transition, the critical part of a speed run. Falling into that wall would not be pretty, but the wall was there. Two months later on a slightly different track the outrun passed through a field of boulders which we padded with straw bales. There were often photographers and spectators very close to the track. Later in Italy, when I had learned through experience and observation what happens to the human body out of control at those speeds, I remembered the wall and the boulders and the spectators at Portillo. I realized how sincere had been our faith, how profound our ignorance, how selective our focus.

For several days we worked tirelessly in the hot sun—shoveling, packing, raking and sweating.

The timing apparatus which had been promised us for a few days of practice was late arriving. Funk, Barrymore and I were inordinately, intolerantly, ungratefully upset over the delay. When Sergio Navarette arrived with the timing we spoke of tying Sergio to a toboggan and letting it go from the top of the track, but at least the timing was in Portillo. Single-mindedness has the unfortunate tendency of damaging tolerance and understanding of life outside the narrow band of that focus. That same day it snowed and several days of work disappeared in the company of our spirits.

Another pattern emerged.

Journal, July 27, 1963:

I have detached myself over a period of several months for this thing. Now I am prepared and we must have it. Without it I will have a difficult time attaching myself. To myself.

Journal, July 28, 1963:

Two letters on my bed tonight were the worst I have ever had. Mother writes that Marcelle has cancer and only days to live. She may be dead by now. Dana wrote to tell me that Tiger Jackson was killed in a gun battle.

I made it a point to see both of them before leaving Reno. Our accounts were square and we were on the best of terms. For that I must be thankful, but I feel so sad I would cry if I knew how.

I never wrote Tiger or Marcelle as I planned and promised. Now it is too late. Right now I am rigorously aware of the shortness of time and the importance of those few ties a person like myself (and Dana) allow to matter. It is certain that I am a better man for having an aunt like Marcelle and a friend like Tiger. To lose both at the same time is numbing.

The world is no longer so fine a place. It is a little less grand and a bit more sad.

Life and people and love are not static...they are forever altering and vanishing...but it is not always easily accepted.

Marcelle and Tiger became a conscious part of it.

Journal, July 31, 1963:

Night. I'm more tired than I've been since I got on the boat in New Orleans. But this is a better fatigue. Today was the best I've had in Chile this year. Barrymore woke me early and said it was going to clear. It was cloudy at the time but he was right. We ran the trap. I have five runs, including the first, and I have not had so much fun in a long time. There was no timing devices so the primary purpose was fun...Tomorrow I leave, but I'll be back and we'll see what we can do about a record. I'm very excited and completely confident. There are moments of fear, but I'm handling them.

The next morning we ran with the clocks. I had three runs between 132 kph and 145 kph before catching the afternoon train to Santiago. The timing equipment was needed for the Chilean National Championships and the Kandahar of the Andes. I had to return to my job as a ski instructor, but we left Portillo with more knowledge of what we were involved with and my notes reveal confidence that one of us would break the record.

．　．　．　．　．　．　．

During that week, while our energies were devoted to speed, word arrived from Cervinia, Italy that Luigi DiMarco's record of 163.265 kph had been raised to 168.224 kph by Alfred Plangger, an Austrian. Raising the goal was not particularly dismaying, but the news that Willy Forrer had fallen and been seriously injured was. None of us knew DiMarco or Plangger and we were sure the Portillo track was best, but we all knew the giant Willy Forrer, whose strength, courage, size and downhill results (1st in the Hahnenkahm, 1st in the Harriman and 4th in two FIS and one Olympic downhills) were legendary. Even giants are human and fall, a fact creating nervousness in the all too human ranks.

. . . .

Two weeks later Ron broke re-broke his ankle at the finish of the Chilean National Downhill at La Parva. This was a blow to the project and devastating to Ron, but we discussed it thoroughly and decided I could handle any organization or work that Ron couldn't. C.B. went to Argentina for a series of races but agreed to return and run with me. Thanks to the unflinching cooperation and support of Racloz and Henry Purcell, the manager of Portillo, I was free to leave in a few days for Portillo. We were one less but the race was still on and Ron could and proved to be invaluable. I was amazed at how well Ron accepted his fate, and I wondered what those circumstances would do to me. In another country less than a year later I was to find out.

We took Ron to Santiago and settled him comfortably into a hotel with amigos, amigas and other amusements and I headed back to La Parva in time for the longest, hardest snow storm I had seen. For two and a half weeks it snowed. There were breaks in the storm and even a cloudless day or two, but they only raised false hopes which crashed into the structure of falling snow. My social life during those snowbound weeks is a fine memory of living in and for the moment, hypersensitive to the nuances of relationships, both close and distant. The speed run underlay it all. I had attained a high degree of a certain form of mental and emotional discipline to go along with the more obvious physical disciplines. 'Abstraction' is the word which most objectively defines the form. My notes show a concern with giving, though once a journalism major and always an American I use the vernacular of money.

Journal, September 1, 1963:

If ... the price of great work is even as high as Van Gogh was forced to pay it should be paid. I'm sure that despite his miserableness Van Gogh would rather have the life he had and produce the work he did than to have the love and family he so desperately wanted and to have been an art dealer without creating art.

Everything contains its own price and the price for excellence, especially in seeing and understanding, is harsh. The price for genius can be brutal and terrible. Regardless, if it must be paid it must be paid.

Journal, September 8, 1963:

A beautiful day, a good, God damn beautiful day.

Nearer, my God, to Thee am I...

I've felt so good today that it is sufficient to say that it is a good, God damn day.

. . . .

Stan Getz, the great jazz saxophone man, once recorded a song titled Nearer, My God, to Thee." The refrain from that piece had been slipping into my mind for a couple of weeks, one of those mental voyages like the journey of the eye following the line of a ridge against the sky, perfectly seen but not defined. Getz music. Getz once said, "My life is music, and in some vague, mysterious and subconscious way, I have always been driven by a taut inner spring which has propelled me to almost compulsively reach for perfection in music, often—in fact mostly—at the expense of everything else in my life."

Nearer, my God, to Thee.

One day that summer the artistic succumbed to the scientific and I thought of the title of the song. The music left and only the title remained. The words appear in my notes and rambled around my thoughts more and more as September progressed.

Journal, September 10, 1963:

The day after tomorrow I go to Portillo. This time, the last time, the speed run is for keeps. I am ready to play for good now and I am confident, though aware.

I believe in the Fates, implying God, but not the one of the churches, and I have thought there may be a reason He is allowing me such a knowledge of myself and honest communication...right now. No matter what happens I have known love and honesty and I am happy.

Whatever happens at Portillo I am fatalistic about it and anything is okay. If the Fates are making a deal with me then I'll live up to my part. Who knows, perhaps I have paid in other ways and the record shall be mine as well as my present happiness. If so, I will understand something more afterwards.

The mind, as well as the body, has its needs: those of the body are the basis of society, those of the mind its ornaments." Jean Jacques Rousseau

And the spirit, Monsieur Rousseau, what of the spirit?

And then Funk was at Portillo hobbling around and skiing on one leg, and C.B. returned from Argentina, and the weather had cleared, and I returned to Portillo, resolved, committed and tuned.

Afterward — Dick & C. B. on the terrace at Portillo

CHAPTER FIVE

The essential education

FREEDOM IS A DIFFERENT CREATURE to every man and in logic there
is no absolute freedom. In reality, it is possible to be free. I have found
freedom in a perfect run for speed, short as it is by conventional terms
of time. A perfect run is when the track is right, the weather clear, you
have held your position throughout and the enigma of balance has been
solved automatically. You have put your head down and rolled your body
into the smallest form you know how to make. You have turned fear to
your advantage. Your body, mind, emotions and skiing technique have
each passed for the moment through its own swamp. Your whole being
is concentrated on one point. You have become a fine tuned instrument
of your finely tuned will.

Words like 'perfect' and 'absolute' leaves one using them in the position of making difficult moves with little protection, and when a run in
big speeds is less than perfect you are only scrambling for survival. And
you will do anything to survive. That is not freedom.

There is a point in big speeds when feelings and impressions (experience?) break through the acquired limitations of skiing. At one speed
you are involved in a fast, bloody tough sehuss, and a few kilometers
faster you are hurtling through space as if time didn't exist. A quiet, insis-
tent roar accompanies you. If you have maintained position you have
surpassed your own limitations. I have known happiness there.

. . . .

John Lyder and Ken Barnes were 18 and 19 year-old Reno boys who loved to ski. I did not know John very well but he was one of the better young Reno racers who looked up to me as a name in local skiing. Kenny was a particular friend. He was five years younger and naturally lived in a different social/cultural world, but I taught him how to select skis and I suggested and loaned him books from my library. The first two were Kipling's "Plain Tales From the Hills" and Hemingway's "The Green Hills of Africa."

We hiked up the slide path on Slide Mountain outside Reno in the summer of 1962 and we talked about things going to hell and about Europe and about skiing. He had been lifting weights in the YMCA and Ken learned on that hike that weights prepare the body more for lifting them than hiking in the mountains.

Ken Barnes was an adventurous spirit and he was honest. His dream was to go to Europe and race on the European tour. He was my friend.

. . . .

The morning of the 11th I went to Portillo by bus and train. In my mail that morning were two letters from my parents. I opened them according to postmark. The first told me that Ken Barnes and John Lyder had visited, talked about their forthcoming trip to Europe and asked how it was going for me. The second letter contained a newspaper clipping reporting their deaths in a sand slide at Lake Lahontan, 50 miles from Reno.

Journal, September 14, 1963:
Tired and sun-drained after two days of hard work on the speed trap. I pack and shovel without a shirt, and it gives me joy and pride and a definite goal to sweat and toil in the sun until I'm out of energy. The work is clean and hard and the run in poor condition. The entire thing is good for me... I'll learn every inch of that run before I go down it, though that is not really necessary.

My confidence is better than when I came. However, it is exacting its price. I find myself edgy and short with people and intolerant of Chilean waiters.

Ken Barnes and John Lyder were killed in a sand slide at Lahontan. They were digging in the sand. No one will ever know why. Just 3 or 4 days before the two of them had been by to see my mother and tell her about their trip to Europe. They wanted to see me there and they wanted to know how I was doing. I was doing fine and I hope they took pleasure in that. I also hope they were knocked out and did not realize they were smothering to death.

I feel Ken's death painfully. I realize how much he would have given to be where I am with the future possibilities I have. I feel heavily my luck in life, and there is, I hope, at least some responsibility toward what I'm doing.

I wish Ken could have had his trip to Europe—he had earned it—but it wasn't allowed him. There is nothing I can do but part of the speed run will be consciously for Ken Barnes. It will be for many, many other people and times and places, conscious and unconscious, but part of it will be for Ken. I hope he knows it.

Journal, September 15, 1963:

Conditions are becoming slowly better and everything is getting closer. Nearer, my God, to Thee.

And a truthful moment or two.

Notes: Every generation should improve upon its predecessor. It should not imitate. That does not mean that each generation should wrap its food in more sterile cellophane and put more horsepower in its cars. Each son should have more tolerance than his father and less waste and frustration, and he should know more about being happy.

That is not how it is, but that is how it should be.

Courage and imagination are necessary for change. Few have either and fewer both.

I'm very harsh on myself and everyone else. I don't like it but I'm mentally honed down and there is no give in me. Portillo is situated so solitude is nearly impossible. Right now I need some solitude. I need a good woman to rub oil gently on my back because it is burned. I need many things.

Journal, September 18, 1963:

It is morning while I wait for the snow to soften so we can work on the speed run. With luck and work we will finish today. If so, practice will begin tomorrow. I'm confident. Just the sight of the monster thing excites me. It is necessary that I succeed over it. My life will be less by far if I fail.

Only a few hours a day are good for working on the run and they are the hottest hours. My face is like an old, used, dried out saddle girth. My mouth and nose are very painful and I look like a leper. It hurts the most when I smile (that's something with my big mouth) and naturally everyone does their best to keep me amused.

Now I am resting and will stay away from the sun and the truly difficult work. Whatever strength I have will be needed, it is not to be sapped to no purpose. The power of the sun at this altitude (over 3000 meters) is amazing, sometimes uncomfortable.

Ron is cutting marker flags and I write here. We listen to snow melting off the roof. Today is Chile's national holiday. There is a festive, gay mood throughout the hotel. For many, however, there is an undercurrent of tension and I have noticed C.B. and myself as well as the others are too quick to laugh, too ready to let loose tension. There is a need for release...the inner tension that leaps at every chance to laugh, to release, to live and love.

The human mechanism doesn't change, only the triggers do and the circumstances.

Journal, September 19, 1963:

In the morning the speed run was ice and rough. I was so bad that Funk remarked, "Remember, Dick, if you don't want to run you don't have to. You're under no obligation." I assured him there was nothing I wanted more. In the afternoon I went out and ran from the highest we have been and went the fastest and had no trouble.

Journal, September 21, 1963:

Another drab day. Studied Spanish, played chess, began Martin Eden and gave a ski lesson.

The timing is supposed to be here tomorrow but I have no faith and feel bad about the whole thing. It is a fiasco and I blame Sergio mostly.

Last night I listened to good music and I miss good jazz and being able to lose myself in the sounds of a noble spirit. If nothing else, America gave birth to the best of all music. I miss that music. How fitting I do not miss the country, only its music.

The United States was a good country and its people had the spirit of life when the music was born. Two wars with a depression in between ruined it. The people were not strong enough, they had no faith, and the land lost its spirit. It will live a long while on its initial values but it will never be what it should have been, and it will one day die or evolve into a thing unrecognizable.

Journal, September 26, 1963:

For the third time the speed run was in shape. I had one slow run and went in for lunch and afterwards it snowed and blew. Tomorrow the entire affair must begin again. My faith is gone and it is very frustrating. There is a similarity in this speed run and being married to an American woman— no matter what you do, or in what faith, or for what intent, it does not matter. It is not enough.

Journal, September 28, 1963:

Late afternoon and as tired as I've ever been. I had four runs on the speed trap today. Right now the times are being computed but I know for sure I had two runs at 156 kph. That's as fast as I've ever been on a pair of skis and the sensation is terrific. I'll never forget it, nor do I want to. Using the vernacular of Ron, I must say that today I saw, accepted and mastered a moment of truth.

The pressure at that velocity is unreal. To do such things it is necessary to be strong, which I am, and it is a blessing that my legs are as they are. Twice my right arm was blown out to the side, and each time it took all my strength to get it back in. this slowed my speed and added a bit of adrenalin to my adrenalin filled moment of truth.

Tomorrow, weather permitting, we go up again after the record. I must rest as I am very tired and I must be psychologically prepared tomorrow. I am physically tired also.

Right now I think C.B. was a little faster than I. Whether or not he was I am quite proud of my red-headed friend today. He was very scared this morning but he kept going up as I went up. He did not like it but he did it.

There is a saying: 'It is nothing to be afraid and not do what you're afraid of, and it is nothing to do something you're not afraid of, but to be afraid and do it anyway that is something.' Today C.B. was a brave man and I am proud to know him.

I'm especially happy for Ron. No matter what happens now—the weather is turning bad again—Ron is off the hook financially, morally and personally. We have done enough to write a story, give advertising to Head Skis and Portillo, and we have lived up to our intent with integrity.

This is the best day I've had in Chile. Tomorrow may be better. I had better sleep now. I don't think I've ever been so tired.

. . . .

The process of detachment—of viewing myself abstractly—had reached an astonishingly intricate, fragile state. I was in an incredible state of mind. Fear, desire, frustration, the scope of our attempt, and pure physical and mental exhaustion had combined to wind me up so tight, so fast, that the contest was not as much with time as whether the record or the human mechanism would fall first.

The next day, the twenty-ninth, was the last day Portillo would be open, the last possible chance for the record. Accordingly, we decided to go up early in the morning and run while the track was still ice. We were sure ice would make the difference. With one day, perhaps only one run left in us, it was necessary to extend ourselves. Sleep the night of the twenty-eighth was restless and unfulfilling. Fatigue sleep of a job undone.

We rose early, ate, and were out on the hill while most of the hotel slept. It was cold and clear. The shaded track was rock hard. Springtime frozen corn; it would remain firm for several hours. We had prepared the track perfectly at the end of the previous day. For the first time, every condition was in our favor.

We took a practice run to test the timing from 20 yards above the measured area. We averaged more than 100 kilometers per hour, and I knew in the center of my spine our track was as ready as we. I would not allow the thought that it was more ready. I remembered what Reddish had told me many months before.

The sun began to climb the track. C. B. and I went with it. Because of the steepness, 400 meters takes great amounts of time and energy, and I was very tired. We climbed slowly, planning to reach the top before the sun exposed the entire track. I felt C. B. had more energy than I, but that may have been hypersensitivity to my own state.

We talked and joked, but the next day we could not remember any of it. When we got to the top the sun was on the track. Portillo was awake. Far below—an impassable distance—people came out to watch. On the hotel porch many had binoculars. Skiers came down the plateau and stood off to one side near the bottom of the track. Spectators of a play in which the actors had not learned their parts, an audience removed, but only on the surface of action. They feared and hoped as did we. Difficult to realize at that moment, but we needed and used their positive energy; for it is true that each is a part of the main.

In that critical state and time, reality was C. B., the gigantic track below, the feeling of vertigo, and the hard knowledge that the next few minutes were the culmination of all that was behind, the determinant of much of what lay ahead. Funk, Purcell, the timers, other racers and many friends were down there watching with varying degrees of interest and involvement; our friends; warm human beings with whom we had formed close and not so close relationships, laughed, danced, drank, gotten angry, forgave and were forgiven; our immediate companions in eating, sleeping, working, relaxing—life; but at the top of the Portillo speed track, those people might as well have been on another planet. All living, except my reality, was suspended. They could not really understand the high degree of control we had made from the chaos of our feelings, nor our predicament, nor the mind which equates self-abstraction with being near God. They could only see us as tiny figures on a white wall of snow, but the least thoughtful could not help but realize our commitment.

I was nearly sick with vertigo and fear. We did warm-up exercises (a delicate task on a slope of 80 percent steepness), and in those last minutes I discovered a bit of the structure of action. The months of discipline, work, self-abstraction and the winding-up process, honed to a fine, sharp edge by the last run on the last day under the iciest, most difficult, most perfect conditions enabled me to see myself marvelously clear.

I nearly laughed and would have but for physical fear. A great calm and confidence (not in success, but in my self) filled me. "Duped again," I would say in a later time. I was at the precipice of the fastest skiing ever done, the fastest a human body had moved without free-falling or mechanical aids, hanging on the side of a snow-blasted cliff, stinking with fear and the stubbornness not to be beaten by it, when I saw the absurdity of my position. Many things had put me up to where I was—whatever it was in my inherent personality that caused me to recognize skiing as my form of expression when a young boy had put me there, and a racing potential which eluded my best efforts. And a public school education with its accent on grade rather than content. And the power of the great yellow lie called journalism which warps the world's mind with its pretension and shallowness. And the Hollywood ethic upon which I was weaned, an ethic preaching that what matters is coming through in the end—a barely disguised belief in a better life after death which makes light-headed excuses for lifetimes of misery. And people like Number 7 who wage war on the past with inverted minds. And all the sweet experiences that had gone to hell. And Beattie with his clumsy feet and blind assurance. And all the teams I and others would never make. And all the old racer friends like Marvin Moriarity and Gardner Smith and Jim Gaddis who had been caught by the sharp, sly, double-edged axe of politics, wielded by the universal soldiers of my particular way of life; but there was also the strength that learning about those kinds of things gives. And there were the good examples of how a man should be; I had once categorized them according to three fine competitors—Werner, Miller, and Buek. There was Funk down there taking pictures; broken leg and all his hopes. There was Marcelle, dying the hard way. And Barnes, Lyder, and Tiger, already gone. And my parents, who never understood but took pleasure when it reached newsprint. There was the good life and people of La Parva. And there were all the friends right there at Portillo. Somewhere in the world was a guy I didn't know named Plangger, and he had something I wanted. And with me was my comrade, C. B. Vaughan. All the people and times and places I had known, and all the shades of emotions I had ever felt, and all the work I had ever accomplished came with me to Portillo. Pushed, pulled, or just came along as disinterested observers. Hard to know, but assuredly there.

And every one of them copped out at the last minute, leaving me entirely, flat alone. Duped again. Abandoned by my own illusions, leaving just me to do whatever was necessary.

The essential education.

The territory my mind had chosen as its battling ground—my place to wage war on all the inequity, hypocrisy, stupidity, and frustration I had ever known; and my time to justify myself for Marcelle, Ken, Tiger, Brett, Brunetto, Funk, Lewellyn, and to my particular friends in Reno, Ron the Mustache, and Joan the Potter, and to a few others for their faith, friendship, and a smile at the right time-was an icy precipitous piece of snow on the side of an Andean mountain, useful in nature only for the tiny bit of water it would hold a little longer. Absurd. Pathetic in its attempt. Yet, something would be saved. Something communicated all around. Duped again, but not entirely for nothing.

I could have laughed.

Inside, where action begins, I was peaceful, confident, and supremely happy. Calm, because preparation gives self-control, and I had come prepared. Confident, because confidence is the only possible state of mind under such circumstances; to be where we were without believing in ourselves would be suicidal, and, while life is richer and more poignant when it is risked (an effect carrying over and preceding the act of risking), it is so through a deep desire to go on living. And happy, supremely so, I say, to discover in that structure mentioned earlier, that life was okay, and so was I; the important thing was commitment, and I found in myself the ability to give everything, to lay the whole show on the line. In that ability is hidden happiness, and all men have it, lurking somewhere amidst neuroses, education, experience and belief, centered in the heart. Success, while certainly not unimportant, is a problematical (mathematical?) afterthought.

While in that delicate, beautiful state, I adjusted my goggles one more time and signaled my readiness to the timers, feeling more than usual action in the center of things. Far below (like looking through the wrong end of a telescope) the signal pole waggled back and forth. I wished C. B. luck, said I'd see him at the bottom. I felt a sentimental reluctance to leave the big redhead up there alone.

"Good luck, Boy," he said. C. B. called his friends "Boy."

I planted my left pole below and to the back of my skis, the right above and to the front, executed a quick jump turn, pulled my poles out in midair, and landed in a full tuck, headin' down.

Acceleration like a rocket launched in the wrong direction. The sound of endless cannons, moving closer. Irreversible commitment.

The soles of my feet said this was the one. My eyes saw the transition and peaceful flat, far, far away. My body, appalled at the danger in which it had been placed, acted automatically, reluctantly perhaps, but with an instinct and precision that preceded the mind which put it there. My naked mind had finally gotten hold of the big one that had always gotten away.

Jesus, it is fast.

After 100 meters I estimate the speed at over 150 kph. That left 200 meters to the timing and 100 meters in the trap before the longed for landing. Never have I wanted more to be finished with something. A few seconds, less than ten—a long way, more than time can record. More than anything, I wanted not to fall. Probably there is little difference in the end result of a fall at 150 kph and one at 170 kph, but the ice that morning accentuated everything that was happening. Acceleration.

Sound. The beating against the legs. The texture feeling. The thin line of error.

In big speeds the skis make peculiar movements. On ice they make them faster, harder. Tremendous air pressure pushes the tips up; the skis want to become airborne. You push forward with everything you have. The air pushes up the tips; you push forward; there is a continuous change of pressure from tip to tail of the skis. Continuous and violent. On a good run your body absorbs both change and violence. On a bad run your body demonstrates them. The tips tend to make a curious, fish-tail motion, which, combined with the tip to tail pressure change, cause the ski to pivot slightly underneath the foot. These things are happening to the skis you are riding. Happening as fast as a vibration and with as much power as the speed you are carrying.

While this is happening at the feet the rest of the body is trying to hold a stable, compact, tuck position. Air pressure tries to push you over backward, with a continuous, ever mounting force. If you break the tuck the pressure tries to rip your arm off. If you stood up at those speeds, your back would hit the snow before the thought could come of what a mistake you had just made.

About a hundred yards above the trap, my right arm, as it had the previous day, flew out to the side for some inexplicable reason of balance. It is tremendously unsettling. (The next time you are ripping along one of America's scenic highways at 100 miles per hour, stick an arm out the window.) I jammed both hands forward and down-a high-speed version of what, in another age, was known as the "Sailer crouch," the stablest position in skiing-and rocketed through the trap and into the transition.

Each mile per hour after 95 feels like a difference of 10 miles per hour at half that speed. When I reached the transition I felt more like a Ferrari than a human, and I knew before the timers that no one had skied that fast before. The run-out was easy—gradually extending the arms and raising the body for air drag, and a long left turn entered at about 60 mph until I was able to stop. It took a couple of hundred feet than any previous run.

I stopped. I took off my helmet and goggles. I was alive. The most

alive I had been in my twenty-four years. I felt the sun and saw the beauty
of Portillo in the Andes as never before. My spirit was clean. My mind
could rest content. I had discovered my own structure of action, and I
had acted. For the time, the illusions had been stripped away, and I was
completely alive. Also, successful.

I walked back around the corner and halfway up the flat. Up on
the hill, Funk was jumping up and down with his cast like a club-foot
chimpanzee.

"One-seven-one," he yelled. "Wahoooo," hopping about like mad,
arms waving.

I stood in the flat waiting for C. B. The calm joy I was experiencing
was tempered by anxiety for the big redhead. I was safe in a giant, flat
expanse of snow; I was alive; I was happy; I was tuned to a very high
plane; but it wasn't over until C. B. was safely down, so I waited a little
longer.

Despite fatigue, the aftereffects of hyperadrenalation, anxiety and
realization of the world record with all its attendant hoopla, those few
minutes were the most peaceful, satisfying moments I had ever known. I
knew they would be few, and I knew they were enough.

In ten minutes, the diplomatic "Bobby" Muller and Chalo Domin-
quez, the timers, had reset the watches. The pole waved for "Ceb." He
came in his yellow-black racing tights like a tiger falling off a white cliff.
The sound—skis rattling against ice, wind rippling skin-tight clothes,
and the impact of a body moving through air at 100 mph-carried clear
to the flat; a unique sound impossible to forget, and not a reassuring
one. C. B. rode a tight but high tuck. Twice his arms broke position,
flashing out to his sides and immediately returned. Then, quite literally,
he thundered into the transition and past me on the flat and around the
corner to a stop.

It was all over.

I stood within my peace wondering about C. B.'s time and looking to
see if it was in me to go up again that day, in case his time was faster than
mine. Almost two years later I was to remember that moment; I remembered it because it took that long to understand what that moment, that

question, that impetus in myself was. As luck would have, it was a catechism I was not to face that day.

C. B. was still around the corner, experiencing, discovering, and questioning on his own when Tito Beladone, the Grand Ambassador of Chilean skiing and friend of several years, skied down the outrun to me. "You and C. B. have the same time," he said. The moment was inordinately formal to Tito's vision of skiing, but he gave me a hug, a pat on the back, a kiss on the cheek, Chilean fashion, and his congratulations. He was elated and proud; I felt humble to have a part in giving him that moment.

I thanked Tito and skied down to C. B. I told him what had happened and we had a few minutes together. During those minutes we knew what we had accomplished, and it was a fine time.

Then the backwash of success arrived. The friends, the ones with faith, the interested, the incredulous, and even the cynical and weak doubters, came to say what we already knew. And it was wonderful to hear.

A full day followed. First were two giant slalom races with the best Chilean racers, both won by Vicho Vera. Then came several quarts of pernod and champagne and a particularly fine bottle of 1890 Spanish cognac. That afternoon, evening and night, September 29, 1963, and into the next morning was a hell of a time.

The next day I began to unwind like a top with a 24 year long string. It took two weeks to come down. Good people, pernod, pisco, Chilean champagne and wine helped restore a nervous system that had been stretched, pulled and abused by all that my portion of human imagination could do to it. During the unwinding we met the grandest lady in Chile or our experience, Chavela Eastman de Edwards, whose late husband had been Chilean ambassador to France, representative to the United Nations and founder of the leading bank and newspaper in Chile. The universal mother and the closest thing I have ever had to a grandmother, she took us in when we returned to Santiago and I was in the best possible circumstances when I came down with para-typhoid a few weeks later. She gave what we needed and found what we wanted. Once she hid all my shoes when I wanted to get out of my sickbed against doctor's orders, and she paid all the bills when I couldn't. Chavela gave me a place to be alone when I needed it, for we had done a momentous thing and were suddenly beautiful people. But I needed, as I had never before needed anything like it, time, a place and the quiet to get used to the fact that it was all over. Chavela gave me that and more.

I stayed in Chile nearly two more months, mostly in bed. There were many things tied together only by the fact of the speed record, not its physical/emotional/personal reality. Glory, fame, satisfaction and the like are ephemeral, short-lived and not what they seem. The point was made and won, and lost on the untouchables.

It was over, I thought. I swore never to run again. I thought my ass never again need be put on the line. Later I learned more about lines. And asses. And thought.

C13RO

VG-CR   (140)   (SPORTS)

SANTIAGO DE CHILE (AP)-TWO U.S. SKIERS, INCLUDING ONE FROM RENO, SET A NEW WORLD RECORD SUNDAY BY SKIING DOWN A CHILEAN MOUNTAINSIDE AT 106.5 MILES AN HOUR.

RENO'S DICK DORWORTH HAD HIS EYE ON THE WORLD SPEED RECORD WHEN HE LEFT FOR THE WINTER SEASON IN CHILE THIS JUNE.

HE AND C.B. VAUGHN OF MIDDLEBURY, VT., WERE GIVEN IDENTICAL CLOCKINGS AS THEY SPED DOWN A RUN AT THE PORTILLO SKI RESORT, 9,000 FEET HIGH IN THE ANDES. PORTILLO WILL BE THE SITE OF THE 1966 WORLD SKI CHAMPIONSHIPS.

THE OLD RECORD OF NEARLY 105 MILES AN HOUR WAS SET BY AUSTRIAN SKIER ALFRED PLANGGER ON A EUROPEAN SLOPE.

THE 24-YEAR-OLD FORMER UNIVERSITY OF NEVADA SKIER DID NOT MAKE THE 1964 U.S. OLYMPIC TEAM BECAUSE OF A CASE OF MUMPS HE SUFFERED DURING THE TRIALS LAST WINTER.

A COMPETITIVE SKIER FOR YEARS, DORWORTH SET A SPEED RECORD FOR THE DIAMOND SUN, SUN VALLEY'S TOP STANDARD RACE, LAST WINTER.
RON
BEN FUNK OF SUN VALLEY, ONE OF THE ORGANIZERS OF THE SUCCESSFUL ASSAULT ON THE WORLD RECORD, SAID THERE ARE NO IMMEDIATE PLANS TO IMPROVE ON THE RECORD IN CHILE.

TJK855APD 2 C NM

Another mountain, another track, the same goal

BOOK TWO

Cervinia
1964

Cervinia, Italy, in the shadow of the Matterhorn,
site of the Kilometro Lanciato, the flying kilmeter race

CHAPTER ONE

PARA-TYPHOID AFFECTS THE HUMAN CONSTITUTION somewhat the
way Von Braun's V2 rockets did London. You survive with some damage but there is no question of invading Europe. My plans for going to
Europe to compete in whatever pre-and post-Olympic races I could get
into were abandoned. I decided it was a propitious time to have painful
bone spurs removed from both feet.

Funk and I returned to the United States a few days before John
Kennedy's assassination. My welcome home was a shakedown by federal
narcotic agents in the Los Angeles International Airport. It was a unique
scene with a Nazi odor. I was taken out of the customs line and escorted
and then trapped in a room with two authoritarians of tough demeanor
seemingly convinced of my guilt until proven innocent.

They searched my belongings and person and did their best with
my mind for nearly two hours. I was very tired from the trip and from
my weeks in bed with para-typhoid and perhaps I looked like a drug
smuggler, but in reality I was just a tired traveler coming home from an
arduous journey and I was not amused. They even went through the
pages of my books. One of them held up a piggy bank sock full of small
change amounting to about $10 and said to me, "This is a pretty suspi-
cious (he actually used the word 'suspicious') way to carry money." He
scoured that poor athletic sock for the evil he sought but only found
small change and his own mind. The knowing looks between those two
national safeguards would have been comic on a movie screen or even to

me had I had a bit more energy and sleep. They saw an educated, unemployed ski instructor with all these here books who doesn't teach school and travels in South America. Just the kind to have a little heroin taped to his crotch, a little grass in a hollow book. The worst kind.

Naturally, they found nothing. They let me go with the warning to "keep your nose clean in the future."

I hadn't thought it dirty.

Those two government officials made an indelible impression on my return to the Motherland. Were they turnkeys disguised as third rate detectives or embodiments of the national psyche? Or were they just two of an ever-expanding army paid by our taxes to prowl through people's belongings, spy on people's movements, suspect people's motives and earn the enmity and disrespect of every man who thinks about and treasures personal freedom? Whatever the dreaded narc's ultimate function in our society, these two set the tone of my return home. I was depressed and shamed by my country before I got out of the airport, the Los Angeles International Airport, U.S.A.

Funk, who had gone through customs with no problem, waited patiently for me to emerge and was as baffled as me by the entire episode. Ron went back to Sun Valley. I returned to Reno, arranged to have my feet operated on and waited around my parent's home in an uncertain frame of mind. On November 22, 1963, a few mornings before the operation, my mother, a grand hearted television addict, came into my room where I was reading and announced, "The television says the president has been shot."

Insanity. It couldn't be. An act out of 1865 and 1914, not our time, the era when reasonable, high-minded men of intellect and values were guiding the country with unparalleled optimism. No one would shoot the President of the United States.

But someone did. Lee Harvey Oswald. As we learned so well, Kennedy's murder was a portent of a bloody time in American history reaching the surface, a time, alas, still here. American history has always been written in blood, and, there is nothing in the subsequent historical record to indicate that the future will be written in another medium.

Optimists had forgotten that not many years before Mahatma Gandhi, perhaps the finest human of the twentieth century, was assassinated. And then came Malcolm X and King and another Kennedy and tens of thousands of Americans and hundreds of thousands of Vietnamese in their own country. Somehow, those two narcs in the airport showed me my country's health before it began publicly vomiting on itself.

I was operated on the morning of John Kennedy's burial, and back in my hospital room after surgery I weaved in an out of consciousness and anesthesia accompanied by the TV image of a flag covered coffin drawn by horses down a large, crowded, silent avenue and the sound of the most mournful drum roll that ever was.

The 25 year old man-boy was home with his record, no longer the same, an intruder in his own country, a stranger in his own home town.

CHAPTER TWO

Sun Valley, my favorite town

IN JANUARY I RETURNED TO SUN VALLEY. Marcelle Herz was buried in Reno the day before I left. She had died the long, slow way and her eulogizer, Father Wayne Williamson, told us Marcelle knew for more than a year what her family learned only when she could no longer hold it alone. Marcelle's first thoughts were for her loved ones, her own pain and fear came last, and her pain went deeper than any drug.

Petty are ambitions. Trivial are world records. Hollow is physical courage in the presence of courage of the heart.

After the funeral services I talked with Dodie Post, Olympic skier, protégé of Marcelle's, wife of novelist Ernest Gann, nice woman. We spoke of the example Marcelle set for those around and behind her. Our talk went to ski racing but quickly moved on to languages learned and people known. It was natural to talk with Dodie of languages and people of the world and of Marcelle from our home town Reno. As if ski racing were a means to an end hinted at in conversations between people and the example of a good one who would be missed.

Llewellyn sat with Marcelle during the last days and she was very rattled. She told me Marcelle was really pleased about the speed run and she spoke of it often. I felt strongly that day the unity of blood relatives in time of family crisis and of my membership in a microcosmic family of families into which we are all born.

The next day I drove to Sun Valley with Dennis McCoy and Wendy Allen, the two young Mammoth Mountain ski racers beginning their first year on the national circuit. They were filled with enthusiasm, hope and talent, and each was the best in the United States within a few years. I was charmed by their dreams and persons but I could only view them with nostalgic wonder. They stayed in Sun Valley a few days for some races before moving on to the next race down a road I knew from a thousand crossings, but I was not unhappy to stay behind.

That winter became a great, bubbling gift from my favorite town and ski resort, the only place I felt was home. It became the fullest period of the life I had up to then experienced. In a way I was home from the wars with a medal. I bartended alternate nights for enough to live on and promptly over-extended the potential of my tender, recuperating feet. No skiing for a month said George Saviers, my mustachioed doctor from the mumps of '63, and no question of racing. I gave into the delicate maneuver of living off past psychic earnings, in this case the inner accomplishment of September Portillo.

For exercise and mental/emotional therapy I ran cross-country (classic style as skate skiing did not yet exist) on the Sun Valley golf course. I liked the solitude. As I got in shape I understood better than ever the gliding rhythm of cross-country skiing, the relaxation and accomplishment of propelling oneself across rolling, snow covered country, the lovely mountains of Idaho my vision and company.

For the first time there was opportunity and a free mind to read and write what and how I pleased. There was no school and reports done on subjects easily forgotten, and no deadly dull scientific studies in military science and Medieval European history. It pains the mind to recall such drudgery. And there was no competitive concern with skiing to color every thought and breath.

I was free.

Though I was surprised at the time, in retrospect it is not at all surprising that I soon plunged with all four feet into what romantics term the great love affair with a lovely, sweet, scared dipsomaniac soon cured, and she broke her leg in her first ski race on Dollar Mountain trying to please me.

Mike Brunetto, my physics minded friend from the University of

Nevada, came to ski between semesters. He quickly fell in love with the Challenger Inn soda fountain girl and skiing was good that year, so he did what any sane skier would do—he quit school, got a night bus boy job in Sun Valley and he and I and my lovely friend rented an apartment in Ketchum for the winter. All necessities were easily fulfilled and no hungering need existed (or, at least, manifested) to prove anything external. Sun Valley 1964 was a quiet, happy time full of peace and friends. Strange and new it was to be so happy outside ski racing, but habit is a hard mold and old ways are often not as broken as one likes to think.

After my feet healed I practiced slalom daily on Penny Mountain. I could walk there on skis from my house and sometimes Funk, Jim Scott, Jerry Fuller or Brunetto would join me for an hour or two. Usually I practiced alone and my better runs happened then. I was at my best when doing it for me, not proving, just doing, a difficult mind set to maintain in the heat of competitive athletics.

Some days I skied Baldy. I rediscovered that winter what I had learned and recognized as a boy and then lost for a time in the speed, complexities and emotional tensions of the racing game—the simplicity and freedom which are joy of skiing down mountains, through trees, over bumps, around corners and in all kinds of snow and weather for the plain, wonderful, uncomplicated hell of it all and no other.

Like every other American skier, part of me was with the Olympic team in Europe.

Journal, February 1, 1964:

The boys in Europe are doing very bad so far. They must feel terrible, especially Bud (Werner). I hope they are able to make up for it in the slalom. Werner, Kidd and Ferries all have first seedings. It is my guess they are over trained. Beattie thinks skiing is like football but it isn't; it is closer to golf. Beattie is probably the best football coach in skiing. That is another story... Whatever is wrong with the Americans I hope to hell they get over it by the slalom. They have tried very hard, but then so have the Europeans.

Many racers, myself and some friends included, had been treated unfairly and dishonestly by Beattie and the U.S. racing program. I hated it and setting a record, making my place, did not change it. Even if I had possessed an ability I didn't and was able to win every major ski race in the world I would still hate it and nothing would be changed. Every time I thought about it my mind went into an angry turmoil. What had happened to me continued to happen and still happens today, though the names have changed. It is older and deeper than the '60s personalities of Dorworth, Moriarity, Gaddis, Smith, Beattie, Seven and others, longer than the sport of ski racing, older and deeper than what I knew. Nevertheless, it is wrong. We all, you and me, know what it is and that it exists in each of us and that wrong is always wrong and needs changing. Yes, if it can't be worked out and changed within the personalities and way of life we know then when and where can it be changed. Next door? Tomorrow? If I cannot change it within myself and do the best for the way of life I know, then what good am I? It is like learning that "yes" is meaningless until you know what it is and how and when to say and mean "no." I knew that I couldn't live with hate for the life I loved most. Eventually I learned that no one can live with hate, and I was learning fast. People I talked with didn't help much, but about the time of the Olympics I found this in James Baldwin's *Another Country*, "...we all commit our crimes. The thing is not to lie about them—to try to understand what you have done, why you have done it...That way, you can begin to forgive yourself. That's very important. If you don't forgive yourself you'll never be able to forgive anybody else and you'll go on committing the same crimes forever."

That helped.

Francois Bonlieu (the best free skier I had ever seen) won the Olympic giant slalom after a decade in the game. I noted in my journal:

Delacroix perceptively points out a difference between the French and English character—the French are motivated by glory and dreams of posterity, the English by duty.

This is true and, borrowing from the English because America has their heritage, a perfect example is to be seen in the Olympics. Werner and Bonlieu. American and French. Same age and experience and, it is supposed, desire. When Bud broke his leg he lost his fantastic and legendary dream of glory, the very thing that made him what he was. He continued out of duty toward skiing, himself and his country. Bonlieu won the GS after many years of seeking glory. Bud could not win though he has, deservingly so, the respect of everyone for dutifully trying.

This is not to mean that glory is better or higher than duty. It is only that glory can push one up on occasion higher than duty. It can, I believe, also drop you lower.

On February 8 Bill Kidd placed second and Jim Heuga third in the Olympic slalom at Innsbruck, the first Olympic medals American men had earned in skiing. It was a fine day for skiing in the United States.

Journal, February 8, 1964:

Heuga and Kidd justified today everything, for themselves and for Beattie. I feel very fine about it despite the fact that it will cement Beattie as coach. That is strange in light of how I think of Bob, but it is such a damn fine thing that everything is justified.

I would give much to be able to see Pete Heuga now. He is, I'm sure, the proudest and happiest papa in the world. He deserves to be.

And Stiegler. How perfect that is. (Pepi Stiegler who helped us in Portillo won the slalom.) The slalom has made me happy.

Journal, February 17, 1964:

My slalom is coming as never before. I am far off what is necessary but I can see and feel where it is wrong and I know it can be corrected. The timing is not quite right and the drive is late rather than lacking. Hearing that Jim (Heuga) won the Arlberg-Kandahar gives me a certain desire to race that has been lacking. S— announced Jimmy's win with the insinuation that an American had finally lucked out in a race long ruled by Europeans, particularly Austrians. Everything in this world is placed on a nationalistic level. The Teutonic people are the worst (best?) at this because of their self-lauding stems from an assurance of superiority rather than from a natural pride of surroundings and life as one is familiar with it. I hate nationalism for the destructive lie it necessarily is. War is, of course, the end result of nationalism. That is where it all finishes. It all begins with fences between neighbors. Frost's poem "Mending Wall" portrays the beginning. Mailer's "The Naked and the Dead" portrays the true ending. Part of the sadness in life is that people do not see any relationship between, for instance, the Olympic Games and World War II or, more important, World War III.

A television company wanted C.B. and I to run for speed against all comers. Challenging matches at 100 mph on the Portillo track. A little like teams of climbers having races up the north face of the Eiger. Absurd. I turned the offer down, though both Funk and C.B. bargained over it for several months. It came to nothing. I refused because I did not want to compete with men as well as mountain on the speed run, but the following appears in my journal:

Yet I have a need to put my life on the line. Perhaps to justify that life. Perhaps to appreciate it. Perhaps to realize it. Perhaps because there are periods when I just don't care that much about it.

Skiing was becoming more personal, a less ambitious endeavor, a seeking within rather than a demonstration.

Journal, February 28, 1964:

The day was good. Two hours of slalom with mistakes coming from ambition rather than lack of skill. There is a difference and I am skiing well enough to know which is which. My satisfaction is great in the actual task of practice and improvement and the ceaseless problem of maintaining and perfecting (to my own limits, for that is all a man can do) a skill. In the sense of art for art's sake I am skiing simply to maintain a skill I don't know what to do with but am not ready to forsake. Will I ever be ready to quit it? I must, one day, no matter how I feel.

Al (an ex-Olympic skier) told me he was unable to train or involve himself completely in his skiing unless he had a definite goal in mind. I had told him I would never make a team in this country no matter how well I skied. Al's definitive goal was making a team. He did. I am barred from definite goals in skiing but that is not sufficient cause to quit. The fact of skiing itself is enough, and certain times I have had on skis is as close to being at one with myself as I have ever come. There can be no doubt that I am a skier, whatever that may mean.

Al is a true and good man and I respect him for that and for his skiing. His philosophy of a definite goal is only the American way and, after all, he is an American. The American philosophy sells life short. It trades life for economy and society. They call it civilization but it isn't. It is barbarianism. Any time the individual is sacrificed (sold out—by his own hand or others is not important except to the individual) for the sake of the whole it is barbarianism. The Aztecs cut out their victim's hearts. The Americans cut out their victim's spirit and in the case of the male cut off his balls. Not, of course, literally, but practically. That is the American (modern America, for it was not always that way) mode of life: to do nothing literal or true but anything, and I mean anything, if it can be called practical. Practical for this barbarian, impersonal society we call America which sets the pace for the world.

Yet, what would Al, for instance, say if I told him he was a barbarian who had lost his spirit and balls to an impersonal and vicious society? Certainly he would never understand or even be close. Probably he would never speak to me. What is tragic, by anyone's definition of tragedy, is that I would not blame him.

It is clear from these notes that I was a perfect candidate for the "turn on, tune in, drop out" culture and ethos that was beginning to form in American society in reaction to and rejection of all the American values that soon led it into the quagmire of Vietnam. (It is worth noting that at this writing—2011—those same values of the same society have enmeshed America in the doomed debacles of Iraq and Afghanistan.)

CHAPTER THREE

Restlessness and the road

A HAPPY, UNLONELY WINTER. Strange, wildly domestic thoughts echoed through my brain and scared me restless. In response, I resorted to the old habit of racing which in me had covered a need older than the eye or ear or mind of man. Time to move on.

Late in March some money came that was owed me. In two days my affairs were in order and everything packed. I said goodbye to my beautiful friend on crutches with the saddest wildcat eyes the day I left, promising to work something out for the future, and Funk and I were off to Aspen in his Chevrolet station wagon called "The Dinosaur" in honor of its specific functional design and packaged obsolescence American cars in general. But it moved and we had caromed along a hundred miles before woman sad eyes and unlonely nights and the hell of it all gave way to the races ahead and old friends and Aspen times and to the highways of America that have no end. We acquire wisdom with age, and it takes ten thousand miles of knowledge to produce one inch of wisdom. For some it takes a hundred million miles to produce even less.

We stayed at my aunt Esther's haven for infidels crossing Mormon Land in Provo as we had a hundred times before, phoning ahead so the best home cooked meal half way to Aspen from Reno or Sun Valley would be ready and hot. Esther fed us, gave us beds, cheered us, opened her home and heart to us and asked where we were going, coming from, doing, thinking and feeling, as she had a hundred times before. Her questions helped me see that my excitement about racing was less than my desire to see people and places I knew and loved. Ron's balding head (Melonhead was one of his nicknames) was showing strains of grey and he was 30 and there was nothing ahead for either of us in American ski racing.

We went to Aspen to stay with that beautiful, hip man Don Lemos. I was lonely for my cat-eyed friend with the broken leg but loneliness was familiar and Aspen is a great town, the total Americana with everything except race riots and freeways.

Then Ron went to Portland on that endless road and I to Crested Butte to race. The U.S. team was there. Kidd and Heuga saved Beattie's job for him at Innsbruck and he exuded confidence and his famed enthusiasm. It was easy to see he had learned a few things in a hard winter before the Olympics and I liked him better. I roomed with Jim Barrier who had driven from a Georgia army base in an ancient Packard and Rex Carson, just discharged from two years of army duty in Garmisch-Partenkirchen. A few old friends and familiar faces and a lot more new faces.

For the first time in fifteen years of racing I questioned my presence at this ski race. It is a moment and question that must come to every athlete and to all men who outlive their professions. In those races and at the Roche Cup in Aspen the next week and at Sugar Bowl a few weeks later I competed the way one would expect of one who had para-typhus and foot surgery four months earlier. I enjoyed my time if not my results.

At the Roche Cup banquet I talked with Tom Corcoran, an old friend, ex-Olympic skier and one of America's greatest racers (4th in the 1960 Olympic giant slalom). We talked about Chile, the speed run and old men racing. Tom, one of the oldest of them all and four years retired from the circuit, had beaten the entire U.S. Olympic team except Kidd in the Roche Cup giant slalom, culminating an argument in print he had carried on all winter with Beattie about a Beattie aberration called the 'Dyna-turn.' And we spoke of old friends in the west.

Number Seven sat at the same table in a stony, jaw-clenched silence. Mountain American gothic. I wondered what he was thinking and if he knew.

After the U.S. National downhill that year, which Ni Orsi won and Werner placed third, I wrote in my notes:

Ni Orsi certainly justified himself yesterday. Bud is finished and I know what pain that will bring him, just as I know he will handle it as a man, silently, and with more pain than most men ever know. Skiing in America will not be the same without Bud as the goal to shoot at. He was the exciting, fearless downhiller that every American wanted to be. My respect is his; I only wish he had quit with the broken leg.

A few weeks later Bud Werner was dead, killed in his last race with an avalanche in Switzerland. Bud was more than a fine human being and a great skier. He was the leader, the hope, the star of an era of American skiing. An entire stage of skiing evolution in America was worked out within the spirit of Bud Werner. I was part of that era and Bud's death deeply affected me. His pride went deeper than winning or losing ski races, though he had that pride too. He always did what was necessary and did it as hard as he could. And in the weeks following his death I often thought of Bud and his pride and how and why he did things.

The night of the day Werner was killed was the banquet for the U.S. National Veteran Championships (now called Masters) at Squaw Valley. I was invited to the banquet and given a Swiss clock-barometer inscribed "Dick Dorworth—World's Downhill Speed Record—Portillo, Chile 1963—106.8 mph—From the Veteran Racers of America."

I was grateful and touched. I remember watching the sad faced Francois Bonlieu who sat at the head table that night as Lee baker said, "We should all, on our own time and in the privacy of our own thoughts, devote a minute to the memory of Bud Werner."

Every skier and many others did.

The call of Europe

EVERY AMERICAN FEELS THE CALL OF EUROPE, for America is Europe's innocent. The most froth lipped flag waver knows in his heart of hearts that Europe holds an invaluable key to unraveling the great mystery of who he is. What skier doesn't want to know what lies behind names like Chamonix, St. Anton, Bad Gastein, Cortina D'Ampezzo, Sestriere, Val D'Isère, Wengen and Kitzbuhel? And what student of art, literature, life or the Gallic spirit isn't enchanted by the possibilities along that section of the road we call Europe? The rare American loses naiveté, but most in their inner selves wants to taste the fruits of knowledge, lose innocence and return to Europe from whence America began.

From high school times of French I, Victor Hugo, Hemingway, Stein Eriksen, Marilyn Monroe, James Dean, and Jazz at the Philharmonic I had wanted to go to Europe. I started a couple of times but some failure of will or floundering of fate always caused it to come to nothing. By the spring of 1964 is was the logical next move.

I kept my promise to the broken legged friend who was healed by then. We found jobs in Reno, planning to work and save until fall and then go to Europe. We settled in. Read. Wrote. Did those living things people do when they are together and happy. A new and scheduled existence: 8 to 5 Monday through Friday at the difficult and well paying boredom that is construction work. Early rising for an hour of reading. Breakfast. Work. Return home. Complain about the hard day, like people all over the world and with less reason for complaint than all but a minute percentage. A secretary and a laborer, we ploughed through living like normal working Americans, rewarded with exorbitant paychecks which were never enough, yoked by heritage to the Puritan ethic of work which has become drudgery for money in this time of shattering the narrow minded mold, sheep who do not love their work and know the poison of the hypocrite and coward every minute they labor for money alone, oxen walking a circle in a path which must in time give the devoted Puritan a peculiar vision of life. Indeed.

Despite the days of physical labor, after work I went to the University track, familiar from hundreds of hours in other times.

A workout description from my May 19, 1964 notes shows a certain resolution:

10 laps (2 ½ miles)
35 push ups
40 sit ups
55 leg wheels
35 push ups
40 leg raises
200 half knee bends in tuck position
30 push ups
40 leg raises
Preceded by complete stretching and warm up exercises

As if to cleanse the stench of toil for gold with an honest labor of love. And I kept in fair shape.

Weekends were consecrated to Dionysus, a faith observed in Reno with a fervor unequaled by any other town, city, village, tribe or clan in my experience. Reno is my home town, the city of my birth.

Such was life—work, save, love, work out, read, write, debauch with good friends, the kind you know from formative years. Ski racing was a vague notion of the European circuit the next winter if it could be worked around the rest of life, not as a primary goal. In fact, I had no primary goal in which to involve my whole being and I had not had one since September.

Living the eight-to-fives could become comfortable. A man could rise so low in the circle he treads as to lose the ability to see over the rim. I was aware of this but comfortable and oddly content, and strange thoughts of a different tone than in the past dripped into my consciousness.

But a man should not live without primary goals.

And so it would have assuredly remained for several months or maybe longer, with unknown damage to spirit and brain, if a telegram had not arrived in late May. The doorbell rang on a Saturday morning of sleeping in after a Friday night gathering of the tribe celebrating in the temple of Bacchus another week and the hell of it all. My lovely friend went to the door and returned to bed with a telegram from Italy and her beautiful eyes were sad again, full of a woman's ancient fear. The telegram was from a Franco Rivetti and would I compete in the Kilometro Lanciato in Cervinia in July and what would be my terms?

I had promised myself and swore to friends and family that I would not run for speed again. That Saturday morning I said I'd think it over, but that was a lie. Ten seconds after reading the telegram I knew I was going to Cervinia. There was nothing to think over. I already knew what I knew in the center of my being where living trumps knowledge, experience and promises. It took millions of years and lifetimes of evolution to make that center the way it is, and only ego saturated blockheads ignore its magnetic, clear messages.

. . . .

For many years the Kilometro Lanciato took place every July in Cervinia on the Italian side of the Matterhorn. When I was there it was held in honor of Silvio Rivetti, a dead brother to Franco. From thirty to sixty so inclined Europeans and Scandinavians gathered annually to seek or exhibit whatever each feels is lacking, or can find or show in the big speeds. A few seek the record but most do not, wanting the organic competition with the other racers more than an abstract number. Some compete with themselves, others experiment with equipment and body positions. A few big hill ski jumpers use the KL to get accustomed to big speeds, as do some world class downhill racers. In all spectaculars involving danger there are a minority whose nature, personality, preparation or skill do not justify their presence, but they will always be there and they were in Cervinia. A few, my favorites, ran only for curiosity, self-exploration and the hell of it. Most Lanciato competitors were Italian, a fact I saw as going deeper than geographic into the national character and psyche.

. . . .

Journal, May 31, 1964:

Three borrowed Whitman quotes...the first two beautiful truths, the third helps explain a commitment I am in the process of making, one I thought I would never want to make...

> *"Muscle and pluck forever!*
> *What invigorates life invigorates death,*
> *And the dead advance,*
> *And the future is no more*
> *Uncertain than the present,*
> *For the roughness of the earth*
> *And of man encloses as much*
> *As the delicatesse of the earth*
> *And of man,*
> *And nothing endures but*
> *Personal qualities."*

> *"A great city is that which*
> *has the greatest men and women.*
> *If it be a few ragged huts it*
> *still is the greatest city*
> *in the whole world."*

"O while I live to be the ruler
of life, not a slave,
To meet life as a powerful
conqueror,
No fumes, no ennui, no more
complaints or scornful
criticisms,
To these proud laws of the air,
the water and the ground,
proving my interior soul
impregnable,
And nothing exterior shall ever
Take command of me."

And nothing exterior shall ever take command of me. The main argu-
ments against my running again are the exterior philosophies of gain and
loss. Inwardly, only my fear of falling keeps me from a complete desire to see
what else is possible to be done. And fear is irrelevant. You must meet it and
conquer it.

Journal, June 1, 1964:

In trying to ferret out the reasons I want to go to Cervinia I have come
across two: 1.) There is in me a need—like love or sex or drinking sometimes
to blow the carbon out of the nerves—to test myself. To prove myself again,
for to fail is to die. And again?

2.) I want to know men who are doing what I am doing, if only one
small part of what I do in life. Men to whom I can say—not in words, for-
bid that!, but in the subtle intonations of spirit—'You and I are doing great
things and we are comrades in spirit. We are attempting the summits other
men avoid and we understand a part of each other because of it. We are
conquerors of speed and all of us will not make it and we know that and it
makes no difference because we are doing great things and we are comrades
in spirit.

I need those two things so badly that I must wonder if they are not forgotten needs of all men, subdued and pushed into subconscious by our time and civilization.

A record is the death of an attempt, dying as soon as it is made, and I do not want to hide behind my record. It is dead. It is alright to take a few bows over a dead record, but you cannot hide behind its tombstone. You must go on to other attempts or you must quit taking bows.

And I am an egoist who is not ready to lay himself down. When I am ready for that there will be no more of anything. Nothing except silence and emptiness and black.

Journal, June 9, 1964:

Another motivation for Cervinia (I am not shopping for reasons to go. It would be very easy and thus impossible not to go.) I want to prove myself before the Europeans, for they are the final critics on all things skiing.

Journal, June 10, 1964:

I am sure of two things about duty. I have a duty next month in Italy, and when skiing is finished I have a long, lonely duty with paper and pen and typewriter.

Again showing the inadequacy of words. Neither duty is like the one for one's parents or wife or employer. My duties are those of revealing the hidden, bound up, fucked up spirit of one man (myself) and thus revealing to all who care to listen what is within every man alive.

As revelations my duties involve more than setting an example, though that is a part. I must illustrate and educate and most important realize—for myself and for all and any who ever wondered with hope if I were able

Bud Werner was great because his character was stronger than anyone else's. He also had talent, skill, courage and the desire to win. These things made him a great skier. His character made him a great man. He lacked certain qualities of temperament and judgment which kept him from being the greatest skier, but his character in the face of these shortcomings proved his greatness as a man. Even now I can hardly believe he is dead. I suspect he never will be—completely.

Journal, June 18, 1964:

Workout today:

3 laps to warm up

stretching exercises

40 push ups

50 leg raises

70 leg wheels

5 440 sprints in 70 seconds each

40 push ups

50 leg raises

300 knee bends in tuck position

1 lap to relax

Journal, June 27, 1964 (The day before leaving for Europe):

If I buy a farm in Italy I mean to buy it with courage* I don't intend to buy the farm but there is no choice but to look one or two over closely, and when I walk away from the farms in three weeks its owner and all the animals will know I am not afraid of them or their farm. I may buy the farm to prove it.

*'Buying the farm' was the colloquialism we used in that time to describe the act and fact of death.

CHAPTER FIVE

"A faith is not acquired by reasoning. One does not fall in love with a woman, or enter the womb or a church, as a result of logical persuasion. Reason may defend an act of faith—but only after the act has been committed, and the man committed to the act."

Arthur Koestler

THE MOLD WAS BROKEN AND HAPPINESS SUSPENDED. Again. Would the pattern change? Do any patterns ever change? Would I ever know? Who knows? I chose Cervinia. The hour morning reading was devoted to the Italian language. Travel arrangements were made. I was lucky to have been working out and I doubled my workouts and extricated myself, bit by bitter bit, from the yoke, the promise and the tribe.

It upset my parents terribly. My mother, in poor health and never much for understanding what she didn't want to see, was hurt. Father was angry the way fathers get with sons of a different pattern, and he spoke to me only in monosyllables for several days. My six year old brother Louis thought it was great. But my parents were always on my side in the long run, even when they couldn't see it at first. They were wonderful once they recognized and accepted that I was going— regardless of their thoughts and feelings and concerns—the way parents are when they acknowledge both the link and the separateness of their children, that the instinct of their sons leads toward improvement and tolerance and away from waste and frustration. I felt they learned to be glad I was going because going is what I needed to remain myself.

The day before I left there was an afternoon party extending into the night at Gene and Joan (nee Arrizabalaga) Wait's, legal advisor and earth mother to the tribe. The party was not for my benefit and many people there I knew slightly or not at all. I was surprised and pleased when person after person, friend and stranger, approached to wish me luck and to say they sincerely liked what I was doing. A few people with a few well-intentioned words are remembered in difficult times.

Late in the afternoon I visited my parents for the last time before leaving. We had a good talk and my father walked with me back to the car. "I want you to remember just one thing," he said. "The greatest favor a son can do his parents is to outlive them."

I could only nod assent.

        ‘ ‘ ‘ ‘ ‘ ‘ ‘

Funk had been lost on that road we knew so well, but I found him by telephone in Balboa Island the night before leaving. He was truly displeased to hear my plans but he wished me luck.

My lovely friend and I stayed up all that last night drinking coffee, eating and fighting creeping loneliness. We talked until time to shave, shower and catch the early morning flight to San Francisco and wait three hours for a flight to New York. Once again, it was time to move on.

On the New York flight I sat next to a young woman just beginning her Peace Corps training. She had never been out of California and thought joining the Peace Corps was the best thing she could do with her life right then. I told her how often I'd driven across the land we were flying over and how long it took from the coast to Salt Lake and Denver to Chicago, and I told her what I was doing was the very best I knew to do with myself. We talked about the sincere and fake Peace Corps people I knew from South America, and she assured me she would be a good one and I know she was. I promised I would hold the best tuck I possibly could for the same reason she would Peace Corps peace into the world with all her heart and mind. I wish her name were still with me.

After I was aboard Alitalia at Kennedy Airport I discovered what I suspected before—C.B. was also going to Cervinia. He was late for the plane and when he boarded we shook hands and said hello and didn't have a chance to speak again until the next morning when we landed in Milano—Europe.

Journal, July 16, 1964:

The Matterhorn is beautiful. It rises above from where I sit like a snowy rock palace of a very personal God. It is easy to understand why it is the best known peak in Europe, though others are bigger and other still more spectacular. The Matterhorn has a personality. It seems to brood and stand in pride (an example?) of its personality and unique beauty. From Cervinia you do not see the profile that is in all the pictures. From here is the rough side, its strength and foundation. From Zermatt you see the Brancusi side. Each has its own personality and there is no use preferring either as the Matterhorn is an entity, like a person, and thus complete because every view is not the same. And, like a person, only one side can be viewed at a time.

CHAPTER SIX

An American at home in Europe

CERVINIA IS A HOTEL VILLAGE in a deep, green valley at the base of the German named Matterhorn. The village is called Breuil and the mountain Mont Cervin in French or Monte Cervino in Italian. Cows graze on the green hillsides, their neck bells creating alpine music from which there is no escape. A long aerial cable car ride above town is the glacier of the Plateau Rosa, some summer ski lifts and the track of the Kilometro Lanciato which wanted the speed record back from Portillo. Cervinia is a quiet place in summer except on weekends when tourists arrive by busloads to look, crowd the streets, sing, drink, eat, be in the mountains and out of the cities and, like weekend tourists everywhere, disappear on Sunday afternoon.

I was at home in Europe from the first day, my mind more occupied with things European than with the action of big speed skiing, and I soon perceived an essential difference between Europe and America to be that of the transient and the permanent. But one night in St. Vincent, not far from Cervinia, after a long dinner with good people a record of Louis Armstrong singing spirituals was played. "Nobody Knows the Troubles I've Seen" particularly moved me and I was pleased to hear it over dinner in an Italian mountain town restaurant.

Armstrong and his music and life embodies something of permanent value in America, and, symbolically enough, on July 4th I heard him again. We had skied all morning on the Plateau Rosa before climbing the Kline Matterhorn for the spectacular views of the Matterhorn, the Breithorn and down the glacier filled valley to the Gonergrat and Zermatt. Afterwards I was invited for lunch in the Yeti Bar by its proprietor, Silvio Alfieri, a high-spirited count by birth whose family paid him a handsome stipend to stay in the mountains and away from their more staid social lowland ponds. Silvio's father was Mussolini's WWII ambassador to Nazi Germany, but Silvio lived in Cervinia, spoke several languages and worked as an interpreter and mountain guide and was the town eccentric and friend to world travelers and fellow eccentrics. He had stocked a crevasse high on the Plateau Rosa with fruit, bread, cheese, wine, beer, chairs and a powerful radio. That was the Yeti Bar. I was honored to be invited. Silvio, Nicole Gillman, a Parisienne who a few years later became the wife and later the widow of Pierre Salinger, John Kennedy's Press Secretary among many other things, and I ate and drank and listened to music in the Yeti Bar—Italy, France and the United States celebrated the Independence Day of my country. As we discussed the differences, similarities and connections between our respective countries the music of Louis Armstrong was playing on the radio. I told Nicole and Silvio that Armstrong is said to have been born on July 4, 1900 in New Orleans where the first jazz, America's original art form, was played. We agreed that his birth date was as symbolic as his music was real.

I had seen Armstrong several times in concert, most recently just a few weeks earlier in a Sparks, Nevada casino. And by listening to him in a mountain crevasse in a foreign land, while talking about my country with a French woman who later married a famous American and the son of an Italian Nazi who was very different than his father must have been, I was able to feel and understand my own Americanism more than I ever could while in the imperialistic, greed-driven pollution that the country of my birth has made from the country of my heritage. I saw in the Yeti Bar that regardless of what I felt, thought, despised and loved about the United States I was, truly and irrevocably, of that country and responsible to and for it. An American. Not ugly, I could hope, but American, and because of that my thoughts and feelings of the nation are at least in part a reflection of myself as much as my country. And C.B. and I were in Europe to beat the Europeans. We had taken their cherished record and they were waiting to take it back. This was above board, clean and honest competition. But a strangeness snuck into my consciousness, perhaps because I was as concerned with things European as I was with the small details and bigger realities of big speeds. By running for speed this time—July, 1964—in Cervinia, Italy I was representing my country against other countries rather than expressing myself. I had joined, for the time, that fraternity/sorority of humanity's most unreliable, robotic, brutal and stupid—the patriot. While that Yeti Bar induced state gave me some insight into why Werner pushed so hard and arguably beyond his time and other things of a political nature, I cannot now imagine a worse frame of mind to think clearly and objectively or to act with precision and honesty and instinct. It was no longer a contest with myself and a steep mountain. It was something more complex and far less clean. I represented a government I did not respect or believe in, and who can control thought or action from that position?

A Hemingwayesque fantasy from my journal of that time:

OW: "Do you think," asked the sincere and wrinkled old woman, "that Mr. Goldwater wants us to go to war?"

DD: "Nobody," I replied to the tired face before me, "wants war except, maybe, a few ambitious generals, a few more psychopathic sergeants, and a small amount more of super-patriots who think they are Americans, for instance, before they are human beings, which, of course, is wrong because nobody is."

OW: "You mean the only good patriot is a dead one?" She cackled a sad, brittle laugh.

DD: "Yes. The same might be said of psychopaths and ambitious generals."

OW: "But Goldwater," the old woman asked with a quietness not unlike a young girl's, "will he take my grandsons like they took my sons, and will he widow my granddaughters like they widowed my girls?"

I was humbled and shamed before the enduring sorrow of woman.

DD: "I don't think," I said, hoping I was right, "that Barry Goldwater

*could ever become President, but even if he did and even if we had a war
you could not say it was his fault. He is only one man and one man cannot
make a war, no matter how powerful he is."*

OW: "I suppose so."

*DD: "Even Napoleon did not do alone all the things he is supposed to
have done."*

*OW: "Yes," she nodded her head so slow and sad it had the timeless
quality of the tides, "I guess you are right. If we have another war who will
be to blame? And who do we blame for all the others? My boys," her voice
slightly rising, "never hurt nobody—they loved life and people—and they
took them and they were gone. Who's to blame? Who's to blame?"*

*DD: "I don't know," I said, feeling sick at her pain and at my own
inadequate knowledge of loneliness. "All I know is that no one man—Goldwater, for instance—is to blame. He, or any man, may be wrong or at fault,
but you cannot blame him or any man. It is true that no man is an island,
but it is more true that no man is a continent."*

OW: "Is God to blame then?"

Being catholic, I did not have the heart to answer.

· · · · · · ·

This fantasy was appropriate to the country I represented at no small
risk in July of 1964 while Lyndon Johnson and Barry Goldwater were
campaigning to see who would become President. Though I was not a
supporter of the conservative world view of Goldwater and thought he
and his policies (and political and social followers) would take the country into war, it was the more liberal L.B.J. who less than a month later
invaded North Viet Nam and started the Viet Nam quagmire which
caused many, including me, to examine more closely than ever the meaning and mechanics of patriotism.

My feeling later came to be that it would have been more honest,
therefore fulfilling, to have met all comers for TV and money at Portillo, rather than for national prestige in Cervinia. It would also have
been more lucrative. For in Cervinia as well, the man with the best time

is meeting all comers and the pragmatics of speed are secondary to that hard, cold fact.

I had questions of a more individual nature and my journals dance all around the problem without grabbing hold, for once you grab you must hang on.

Journal, June 23, 1964:

If, when everything is over, your work finished, your loves fulfilled or withered or picked by others, your life lived, your deeds—both good and bad—etched into the past and paid for and harvested, your heart broken for the last time, your head filled as far as it will ever be, your spirit to be no longer compromised without its consent, then where is the reckoning? What the ledger? By what do you measure?

The quality of your actions?

The quantity?

The results?

The intent?

Or is it enough to do the best you can with what you are able to have, and if you do not do your best you are failing? That might be close to the truth. It would mirror life as it is lived by humans, under the conditions they impose upon themselves.

Was I looking for disaster. Had a few weeks of the eight-to-fives prepared me to accept any out to avoid the monotony, the grind, the yoke and the promise? Speed skiing was no longer a goal and the line is too thin for it ever to be my means. Men always pay for false conceptions and for replacing the basic with the transitory, and I was not to be excepted.

I was in fact as conflicted as my country and more American than I thought.

CHAPTER SEVEN

On tracks of different temperaments

THE CERVINIA SPEED RUN is both objectively and subjectively different from Portillo's. The Chilean track measures 400 meters to the transition and up to 80 percent steepness; Italy's is a kilometer long and 62 percent at the steepest point. It starts nearly flat and falls off to about 20 percent for 400 meters; on a good run the competitor is traveling about 60-70 mph at the end of this relative flat; then the contour changes abruptly and drastically, and the rest of the track is a consistent 60 percent. This contour change coincides with a crevasse which is boarded over and covered with snow to allow a crossing. It is impossible to resist being thrown in the air where the track changes. Depending on the individual run, conditions of the track, and, of course, the competitor, seekers of speed fly anywhere from 20 to 120 feet. How the racer masters that obstacle will have an appreciable effect on his time. As in downhill racing, it is faster to be in the air 20 feet than 100 feet; but the most important factor is one's ability to hold the extremely low, tight, body position before the bump, in flight and after landing. Opening the arms slightly for balance will cost you the race. A serious alienation from the thread of balance at this point results in one of those struggling runs that bring awareness of the depth of the will to survive, a realization that casts a glow of understanding on the terror and struggle of rising from the swamp to open air. After landing, the big speeds commence. Up to then, speed is acquired gradually; the racer has time to get into a comfortable, compact position, time to get accustomed to speed, time to get acquainted with the muscles he will need, time to think. In elapsed time, measured in seconds, the racer is on the Cervinia track three to four times longer than in Portillo; they are tracks of different temperaments arriving at the same conclusion. Commitment. Concentration. Freedom. Or the struggle of terror.

There is another crucial difference between Cervinia and Portillo: the transition, in terms of safety the most important part of a speed run. In the transition, speed begins to diminish. The transition is like the first touchdown of a jet, except this jet lands at full speed. It is where the potency of speed, the consequence of commitment, the gyroscope of balance show their hands. It is where gravity, always tiptoeing in your shadow, adds its weight to your passing. As if to see that your legs are as strong as you have committed them to be.

The transition in Portillo goes from a 52 percent slope to a 15 percent slope. You must accept and adapt to a 37 percent change in grade. Gravity does not hit you very hard; it tiptoes slightly behind.

In Cervinia the transition holds you the way a jet taking off forces you into your seats; except this jet reaches top speed much faster. The transition is from a 60 percent slope to a 15 yard flat to a 12 percent slope, but the 12 percent is in the other direction. Uphill. You are confronted with a 72 percent change at over 100 mph. It is a transition that would like to suck you down and break you into a million pieces and spit them out in China. Gravity romps upon your head.

There is a difference between Cervinia and Portillo which manifests itself more in psychology than objective reality. After the racer in Cervinia has gone 200 meters he disappears from the vision of the competitors on top. More than thirty seconds pass before an impersonal loudspeaker on a post at the start announces the racer's time and "La Piste e Libera," the track is free. Sometimes the track is not free. This can mean several things, including a fallen racer. But you do not know because you cannot see; and the starters, in radio contact with the bottom, are arbitrary about what they tell you. Aside from his announced time, you do not know how it went for the previous racer. This can weigh heavy upon the mind.

To this Cervinia we came with our record: big, red-headed C.B., so uncomfortable in Europe that he was back in Vermont ten days after the competition, and travel-struck Dorworth, not paying attention to what he was supposed to be doing but who stayed in Europe for fifteen months. The Americans.

But if I wasn't attentive enough to the content of action I was concerned with the quality of style.

Journal, July 2, 1964:

The track is not nearly ready. My attitude is much different than last year. I know I have done it and I am confident I can do it again. I am not here to beat times—I think the record is safe from Cervinia—but to beat the others. I am ambitious and confident. If I have bad luck it is only that and nothing more and has nothing to do with anything truly important. The same with good luck. What counts is the attempt and the manner of it and one's conduct.

I wish I were not lonely. Loneliness takes my strength and yet gives it back in another place. That is not unusual. Great things have been done by men hollowed out by loneliness. Not happily for them, perhaps, but if the work counts more than the man then it is justified.

CHAPTER EIGHT

Luigi

LUIGI DIMARCO WAS MORE DEDICATED to the pursuit of pure speed than any other skier of that time. In 1964 Luigi was 27 years old and had only skied for eight years, but in that time he had won and lost the world record. A short, muscular, all Italian man with a big, easy smile and hard, clear, blue eyes, Luigi was as fierce and objective about competition as anyone I've ever known. His territory was that realm of snow and mind I call 'the big speeds,' specifically the Cervinia speed track on the summer snows of the Plateau Rosa. And a man who has staked his claim and taken his stand is attuned to the subtleties of that ground to a degree the occasional traveler, intruder, fortune hunter, thief, lost soul, prospector or curious can never reach. Though understandably not the best skier on the planet, DiMarco was as responsible as he was unacknowledged for some major refinements of speed and downhill skiing tucks and techniques, including hands breaking the wind in front of the face and the exaggerated low position with head dropped between the knees. Luigi contributed significantly to the evolution of skiing in more ways than moving up the speed record, and his influence is evident even today in any downhill race.

DiMarco started with the basic positions of downhill and tightened them to a degree previously unimagined, refined them, and then held them during the fastest skiing ever done. Speed skiing was Luigi's bread and butter, the record his motivation, his innovations his legacy.

The first time I saw DiMarco he was atop an electrical pole on the main street of Cervinia helping string a banner announcing the Kilo-metro Lanciato. I had seen photos of him speed skiing but had no idea what he looked like. Yet I somehow knew that this athletic looking fellow on the pole was our prime competitor. I noted that he watched us very carefully, studiously even, in that manner that made me feel like we had something he wanted very badly. I liked him immensely from the first and later that day we met and became immediate friends.

Soon after that I saw him on the speed track and realized he was a master. I had seen masters before: Stein Eriksen in 1953, Toni Sailer in 1957, Christian Pravda for several years, Bud Werner in 1959, Chuck Ferries in slalom in 1962 and 1963, and Bill Kidd in 1963 and 1964, but this master showed me a new realm of competition. C.B. and I jointly held the world record and we had earned it with our own thought, sweat, commitment and will, but when I saw Luigi in big speeds I was embarrassed. The record was mine in fact alone.

. . . .

In 1959, the year Bud Werner was the best ski racer in the world and so far ahead of any other American that in America competition was for second place, Chuck Ferries either beat Bud or came within a couple of tenths of a second (I've forgotten which) in a slalom in Stowe. That was three years before chuck developed into the best slalom skier in the world, and his result was startling enough for me to offer my enthusiastic congratulations. He was embarrassed and said it was a fluke, that he had no business being within five seconds of Werner. He said, "I don't ski well enough to shine Werner's boots."

In 1959 I didn't understand Chuck's words. In 1964 I saw DiMarco and I understood.

. . . .

I became, in the privacy of my own mind, Luigi's apprentice, a worthy one I thought, somewhat impeded by holding the speed record. I was fascinated by the knowledge that in big speeds DiMarco knew with his mind what I guessed at with my will.

But I had solid faith in my will.

Journal, July 6, 1964:

There were four trips on the speed run today. The last two I would judge between 130 and 140 kph. My own skis will be here tonight or tomorrow and then I will go for more. I feel so strong and sure that I am hungry for it, as opposed to simply committing myself to the unknown as I was forced to last year. I will still commit myself if necessary, for my control seems as good as my strength and sureness, but that is an ace to be used only if I lose courage.

The French are not here but I know I can beat DiMarco if my skis are as good as his. If I can beat him I can beat anybody, and my aim right now is to beat everyone in the world in the next two weeks at this particular game.

My faith in myself in this is very good. If I lack faith in certain people in certain circumstances and if this lack sometimes hurts me, well, then, it evens out by the faith I have in what I can do.

Was all that in Chile simply a testing, a training, a warm up?

CHAPTER NINE

Foresight, hindsight, death and mortality

THE WINDING UP PROCESS WAS WELL UNDER WAY though not so intense or important as in Portillo. The confidence and experience gained in Portillo allowed me some objectivity about matters that would have thrown me into angry pandemonium a year earlier.

A few days after arriving my journal reads:

From the vantage point of looking into the future I have the suspicion (more than that) that the people here know less about the fundamentals of speed on skis than I did a year ago. They are interested in a show and they want badly their record back, but the fine details of grooming and preparation are being ignored and those very details are what make records. This is only foresight which is often as incorrect as hindsight is too late. It is also only my own observation, which is often incorrect—and too late.

Death, once again, reminded us of our mortality

Journal, July 7, 1964:

I have just heard that Charles Bozon was killed today in an avalanche in Chamonix. The mountains take back what they give and another man of character is gone and the world cannot afford to lose such men. Bozon was to France something like Werner was to America. They both had character and they both knew disappointment and frustration and the mountains have taken them back.

When greatness leaves this world it is as sad as the death of a child except a great deal more is salvaged.

Bozon was an inspiring skier and person who won the 1962 FIS world championship slalom. He and 14 other French mountain guides had been killed in an avalanche in Chamonix. It had been a hard year for skiing.

I was not superstitious, but I was winding up.

Journal, July 8, 1964:

Had two runs of about 140 today. They were steady and I felt strong but I am disappointed in the manner they are running this event. They are so organized that nothing is done. The clocks don't work. The track is awful. And the many, many chiefs who walk back and forth with their feet on the track speak very often and loud and do nothing. I had a good argument with these pompous officials when they started me, stopped me, let two others run, and then closed the track. I was mad as hell. Later I noticed how unusually quick my temper had been. Perhaps it is the big speeds or the beginning of them. Something similar happened last year.

Journal, July 9, 1964:

A day so good I feel it is far better than many I have called good. We went between 140 and 148 today in all our runs and I have never had so much fun on skis. I feel as if I can beat anyone. Which is, after all, irrelevant. I have tested myself and found myself not lacking. And in the next ten days I will blow a lot of carbon around and I should be clean inside.

Journal, July 11, 1964:

Some good runs today receiving compliments though the watches were not in. I used the 230s and will try the 225s tomorrow. I suspect the shorter ski will be better. I sense the longer ski is just excess wood and there is too much tip to control and that if the binding were moved forward the long tail would drag. We shall see but that is how I think right now.

In Portillo we used 225 centimeter Head metal skis made in America, no different than normal downhill skis except 5 cm longer. The skis I used in Portillo were borrowed from Funk after he was unable to use them. I preferred my own German made downhill skis which were 220 cm which are unsteady at big speeds.

During the two years (1964-65) I raced in Cervinia I tried many Kneissl skis from 225 cm to 245 cm and found I performed best on 230 cm skis, double grooved with one piece edges. This ski was noticeably heavier than a normal downhill ski, the bindings mounted dead center, slightly ahead of the usual downhill binding placement.

Along with the skis Kneissl sent to Cervinia came Egon Schopf, coach for the Kneissl racers. Egon was many times Austrian champion in the late 40s, winner of the Hahnenkahm and third in the 1950 FIS world championship downhill. As a coach he was priceless and it was easy to see that Kneissl valued what we were doing. It was also easy to see the advertising potential for the ski manufacturer with the winning ski, but advertising potential or not (and why not?) Kneissl allowed me to realize for the first time the benefit of organized help in my skiing. Help in Italy from an Austrian firm was a good feeling and it was not the last help I would receive from Kneissl.

Speed skiing made a major step forward at Cervinia in 1964 with the most formidable field ever gathered to that point. The competition included:

Bruno Alberti, winner of the Arlberg Kandahar downhill, retired from racing and slightly past his peak but still the best Italian racer since Zeno Colo.

Ivo Mahlknecht, the best Italian downhiller of the time and ranked among the first ten in the world.

Kalevi Hakkinen, an incredible and durable Olympic skier from Finland who I first met in Chile in 1958. Kalevi was 36 in 1964 and won the KL in 1968 and was still competing in speed races well into his 60s.

From Japan came Yuichiro Miura who had trained for a year for this event. He was accompanied by his father and two cameramen and we became immediate friends. I wrote in my journal:

The Japanese, Miura, gave me a parka for the Lanciato. The parka has SPEED DASH in English on the front and back and is the size for Miura. It is so tight it cuts the circulation in my arms and it is perfect for this race.

The Japanese are very nice and fantastic good will ambassadors for their country. They exhibit the beauty of pride in one's own country. It is sad that the beauty of pride in one's own country is on the other side of a fine line from the ugliness of nationalism. I would like to think of my country as the Japanese do of theirs. It must give them strength and a good feeling, but since I cannot I will try to appreciate those who do.

Miura was an incredible competitor and his two companions made a fine film of the speed run that we saw the next year. In 1970 Miura skied from 25,000 feet on Mt. Everest and the film of that adventure "The Man Who Skied Down Everest" won the Academy Award for best documentary in 1975. Twice in the 21st century Miura climbed Mt. Everest to the summit, the first at the age of 70 with his son and the second time at the age of 75. He is, at this writing, the oldest person to have climbed Everest.

Heini Messner was one of the strongest racers in the world, several times Austrian champion. He won bronze medals in both the 1968 and 1972 Olympics..

Eighteen year old Walter Mussner was the Italian junior champion and had a remarkable facial resemblance to Bud Werner. I had a strong older brother feeling for this tragic boy and I both liked and admired his combined qualities of childish enthusiasm and solid courage.

Roberto Gasperl, son of Leo, who lived in Cervinia and had a wealth of experience on the speed track.

From France came two of their greatest downhill skiers, Guy Perillat and Adrien Duvillard.

All together here were 38 men, 4 women and 12 junior competitors at the 1964 KL. I estimate that a third of the men had eyes on the record and were seriously prepared to win. That is a lot of men with all the strengths and weaknesses of men when the line of error is so narrow as to be invisible.

CHAPTER TEN

Gladiators of speed

THE KILOMETRO LANCIATO was a scheduled, organized competition intended to assure competitors equal and safe conditions in which to compete. Since such events have an uncommon interest to the so inclined spectator there is about it an aura of festivity and tension similar to those surrounding car races, bullfights and, one could easily imagine, the gladiatorial contests held in the Coliseum of Rome during the birth of the last age and the death of the one before.

Competition lasts a week. Each day the racers take as many runs as they can, depending on the individual's speed in getting back to the top of the track (involving a ride up a Poma lift and a long, upward angling traverse), the condition of the track and the luck one always needs in working towards one's own ends within an organization. Six or seven runs is a big day and some days there are none. The track is opened and closed at the discretion of officials. The fastest run of the week wins, but for reasons of competitive psychology and the elimination of the slowest racers each day from the next day's competition the best runs usually happen the last day. Only the serious and capable survive to the last day.

Forty skiers running four or five times a day at 100 mph are hard on a track. In Cervinia, unlike Portillo, the seekers of speed were not responsible for track preparation and maintenance. Both years I competed at Cervinia my strongest and oft voiced complaint was the track's condition. An organized, group competition like the KL is by nature a very different event than what we had in Portillo where we worked for weeks to insure the track's smoothness. Whatever competition existing between me and C.B. (and Funk until he was hurt) was submerged in the joint pursuit of the record, and we chose what day and under what conditions to run according to our own willingness to work out whatever pragmatic problems arose or let them go by. Just two men were involved, not forty, and it was truly more a matter of man against mountain rather than men against men. In Portillo we ran our own show. In Cervinia we were only the gladiators.

. . . .

There are many roads to Armageddon and each person's path reveals personality more than skill. For me speed skiing was a matter of mental and physical preparation and when I had put in the time and effort to condition and wind up I could do it. Like most people, when I am not prepared to do what I am doing it is a vacuum in my being, a deficit in my will, a trapdoor in my luck. I built up to big speeds with a first run never more than 50 mph, beginning low on the track and moving up each time in 20 yard increments. After a few days I could run comfortably from the top and after that each run was from there. No retreat on the objective front.

As in all endeavors, each person's style is unique. C.B. and Luigi worked up the track in a similar manner to mine, though Luigi began his ascent at a higher point on the track. Messner and Alberti arrived at the top in about three stages. Hakkinen, like me, was cautious in the beginning but very strong once accustomed to the speed. Miura was a bit overwhelmed by the size of what he had come halfway around the world to conquer. His first days seemed like tentative feelers on the giant track and he did not appear to be prepared or anxious for the competition, but he soon mastered his deepest doubts.

Alfred Plangger really stunned me. He arrived in Cervinia a day or two before the competition began, several days later than any of the others and two weeks later than C.B., me and Luigi. He said he had not been on skis in three months, which may have been the words of a hard player of the game, but he was not suntanned and did not appear to be in particularly good shape. Nevertheless, the first run Plangger took in Cervinia was from the top of the speed track. To be off skis for three months and to fire your first run at 100 mph is a bold move, but Alfred played hard. I admired his élan but never felt he was seriously after the record we had taken from him.

The field ranged, more or less, somewhere between my caution and Plangger's boldness. By the time each of us had finished our preparations, geared our minds, committed our selves and stood on the top of the track on the first day of competition we were all about the same— give or take a few shades of technique and degrees of will that always separate those who win from those who are left behind, and those shades and degrees tend to shift and change from day to day.

CHAPTER ELEVEN

A day I must always remember

COMPETITION BEGAN JULY 13TH on a grey day with a soft track. Opening ceremonies necessitated the entire field running once from just over half way up. That took time and the best part of the day was wasted.

I was third in the day's competition in which I had the distinction and moot honor and experience of starting first. It was not a fulfilling day.

Journal, July 13, 1964:

A bad day, the first of competition. The best I could do was 160 kph. Yesterday, starting 200 meters lower, I had 163. Today I started higher than anyone, and by the time I reached the two drop offs at the top of the real hill I was going too fast to hold my tuck. I flew 25 or 30 meters off the second jump. Luigi started more than a hundred meters lower than I, as did Alberti, and Luigi had 167 and Bruno 163. C.B. had a fine run, holding his tuck all the way (though his position is too high), but the timers missed his time. He was furious. Nicole said she had never heard such language in English so loud and in front of so many people. I did not blame him his manners, and I agreed when he told them he would pack up if they missed again.

We went up for another try but the weather moved in and the track was closed. Tomorrow I will start where DiMarco does and see if I can hold my tuck through the two drop offs. I am disappointed but I am not worried about tomorrow. I spent a long time talking to Luigi today and I have learned much. He is the most experienced speed runner in the world and he knows Cervinia perfectly. If I listen hard enough to him I can beat him. He knows that and he will not cease to tell me what I need to know; that is an indication of how fine a competitor he is, how good a man.

There is no longer a question of my ability to commit myself to any action. I have solved that and I do not think I will doubt myself (at least so far as commitment to what must be done) ever again. It is a question of holding a good tuck, having the right wax, and, as always, having just a little luck.

In some respects the first day was a portent of things to come. Luigi, Alberti, myself, Siorpaes, Plangger, Messner, Mussner and Hakkinen were in the first ten, and it is sure C.B. would have been. But Miura could only manage 150.000; Mahlknecht 148.576; and Gasperl 142.857; and those times were not indicative of how it would be.

Results of first ten, July 13, 1964

Luigi DiMarco, Italy	167.441
Bruno Alberti, Italy	163.785
Richard Dorworth, USA	160.642
Gildo Siorpaes, Italy	160.427
Alfred Plangger, Austria	159.645
Michelangelo Bosin, Italy	159.645
Heini Messner, Austria	159.574
Walter Mussner, Italy	158.870
Kalevi Hakkinen, Finland	157.894
Luciano Seghi, Italy	157.894

· · · · · · ·

The 14th gave us perfect weather. A hot summer day in the Alps. The track was in good condition. Spirits were higher. Competition had begun. The game was on.

I had listened closely to DiMarco and I started where he started and remembered his words. I held my position and was third in the first round with 161.943. Luigi and Bruno were less than 2 kph ahead. I felt very strong.

Egon and I talked about my run and decided I should switch from 225 cm skis to a freshly waxed pair of 230s. On the next round I had my slowest run from the top of a speed track, barely 159 kph. The others improved their times while I dropped from third to eighth. Miura turned in a surprising 163.562 and it was evident he had discovered his own structure of action. I was disgusted with myself and hurried to the top for a rectifying run, but just as I arrived the track was deemed too soft and closed by the officials.

The day ended like the taste of rancid butter.

Results of first ten, July 14, 1964

Bruno Alberti, Italy	167.286
Luigi DiMarco, Italy	167.053
C.B. Vaughan, USA	164.533
Yuichiro Miura, Japan	163.562
Kalevi Hakkinen, Finland	162.748
Heini Messner, Austria	162.675
Edoardo Agreiter, Italy	162.162
Richard Dorworth, USA	161.943
Gildo Siorpaes, Italy	161.218
Walter Mussner, Italy	161.073

. . . .

July 15, 1964. A day I must always remember, a day that expanded the horizons of my experience, showing me something of myself that only such a day could reveal.

The weather was good and the track in the best shape we had seen. C.B. had a good run the day before and was hungry for more. I had banished my discouragement and felt confident and distinctly remember abundant happiness. As I had told the Peace Corps girl, to be in

Cervinia doing this was the best thing I could do with myself. Nothing was so important to my progress as a man than getting my body down a mountain on a pair of skis just as fast as I could go. I didn't know why but I knew it was so, and it was.

But that superb bitch Fate had a fickle lesson I hadn't yet learned. We were all at the top. The first run began, the timing was not functioning perfectly and the times of several racers had been missed. C.B. was growling about the timers not missing him. Alberti and I posed for photographers. DiMarco had an early starting number, mine was several numbers later. He went but I was not watching. Bruno and I were talking when the starters and the speaker on a post simultaneously silenced us and changed the mood of the day. DiMarco had gone 173.493. The record was his once again.

I felt empty and did not want to talk or look anyone in the eye. It was a private moment. I think it was a private moment for every competitor who was consciously and seriously ready to win. The Italians cheered and shouted for their countryman's success. It was not a good position for the Americans.

I went to C.B. We encouraged each other and readied ourselves to get the record back. C.B. had served his apprenticeship and when he went a few minutes later he was prepared. He went 168.145, a run beaten only by DiMarco, Plangger and he and I in all of skiing history, but it was far short of what was necessary.

Then came my turn. I moved out to the track, acutely aware of that interpersonal pressure I have always hated. What had once been an attempt on my part was now expected of me. At least that was my feeling, as if a heavier load than I ever intended to carry was suddenly mine. But I knew the work well and I had faith in my will.

"La piste e libera."

I began. In relative terms it does not seem much to build up to 20-30-40 and 50 mph when in a few seconds you will be hurtling along at more than 100 mph, but you must pay close attention at those relatively slow speeds. Your mind is absorbed in technical details and there can be no abstract thoughts like records or the game. Your attention must be total.

Perhaps, on that run, my attention was strained.

I rolled my body into the most aerodynamic cone I knew how to make, working the terrain changes with a flat ski to get every wave of speed before the jumps and the steep hill, velocity at the jumps helping determine the eventual speed through the timing trap. I focused down, doing my best.

I flew off the jump but held position and landed with no problem. The big speeds rolled in upon me and I aimed along the right side, the fastest line.

About a hundred yards above the trap the inexpressible happened. That thing you must never dwell upon, that point in space and time to which Perillat referred—"You must not think too much."—had coincided with my run. The thread of balance had broken. It was apparent and inescapable that I was going to fall. I was convinced. There was no fear, only a clinical, sure knowledge. All the time I was trying to avoid the inevitable fall and all the while I was falling there was no fear, only a (detached?) cool observation of the fastest flow of events I had ever witnessed. There is an infinitely fragile line of balance at 100 mph because you are more like a projectile than a skier, and once that line is broken it does not mend easily. About 200 yards remained to the transition and it takes slightly over four seconds to travel that far that fast. It seemed like five minutes and I tried every conceivable adaptation to regain balance—and the line is so thin that spectators didn't know I was in trouble until I actually fell; even C.B., watching closely, didn't know—but only a forgiving god could have saved me and the forgiving gods were busy elsewhere that day. I knew it would expose me defenselessly once I fell, but I was not scared. I tried a hundred positions and a thousand thoughts but I would not be forgiven inattention. Experience breeds a slight contempt for the forces in speed. When I reached the transition it sucked me down just like I knew it would, but I thought I'd try for Iraq in two or three pieces rather than China in a million. As I went down I tried to get on my back and bottom. Perhaps I could ride it out in a long skid as I'd seen ski jumpers do. Now I know that strange things happen to your body when it meets the snow at 100 mph, no matter what the position. In the twinkling of hitting the snow I regained a proper respect for speed. If you are inattentive, as well as somewhat stupid, you may breed a contempt for big speeds in forgetting respect through the grace of being atop your skis each run. No one on his back at 100 mph will ever after have contempt for speed. Something caught—a hand, perhaps, and then came one of those falls skiers have bad dreams about. Eighty yards up that hill rising out of the transition in every conceivable body position including upside down and backward and five feet off the snow. A memorable fall. Visually a blur of snow and sky and an occasional form moving faster than focus, too fast for the eye but not for the mind. The films of the fall pass more quickly than memory impressions left with my mind, for the mind registers feelings, the eye only illusion. The left ski went away as the binding meant it to and was last seen on the way to Zermatt. The right ski loyally stayed and half way through the fall the leg broke. The fall and I finished our relationship and it left me in a pile, alone, as the end of relationships tend to do. I hurt everywhere and I immediately began to review my scant knowledge of physiology. Not until then did I fear (feel fear) that I may have destroyed my body. I once broke a leg that took two years to put back in shape. I flashed on those years. Bad years. I knew my good leg was broken and my body was a pulsing pain. I undid the binding which meant I could move, and fear gave way to the objective mind. My fall deposited me apart from people and it took a little time for them to arrive. My left ski, poles, gloves, goggles and glasses were no longer with me, and the sleeves of the ultra tight Japanese speed suit Miura had given me were somehow shoved up and over my elbows in a wad. C.B. was the first person to reach me. I was happy for that and grateful that he came so fast. He supervised the first aid men when they arrived and I was touched by his concern.

Italians are really prepared for accidents. I was fascinated by the first air splint I had seen, used on my own leg. People were swarming around and by then it was determined that in the relative world of injuries I was alright. There were the smiles and relief of the silence of disaster giving way to the movement of life.

The leg was slightly broken about four inches above the ankle. The muscles in that leg were sprained and torn and painful. My body was a huge bruise, especially my buttocks which were wildly colored for several weeks. Something happened to my back that I didn't notice at the time but for many years after it would seize up and nearly immobilize me at inopportune times.

Two days later I noted:

So, I have a broken leg and tender buttocks. Considering that I made the very serious mistake of falling at 100 mph I am quite lucky.

Results of first ten, July 15, 1964

Luigi DiMarco, Italy	173.493
Bruno Alberti, Italy	169.651
Yuichiro Miura, Japan	169.014
C.B. Vaughan, USA	168.145
Walter Mussner, Italy	167.208
Heini Messner, Austria	167.130
Alfred Plangger, Austria	166.358
Renzo Zandegiacomo, Italy	165.975
Kalevi Hakkinen, Finland	165.441
Gildo Siorpaes, Italy	164.835

. . . .

There was no fear, only a clinical, sure knowledge...all the time I was trying to avoid the inevitable fall, and all the time I was falling there was no fear. Only a (detached?) cool observation of the fastest flow of events I had ever witnessed.

A few years later I came to realize what it is to have your mind and the rest of your existence so far out of harmony. It is one thing to be intelligent, objective, aware, hip to your surroundings; it is something else entirely to observe your own impending destruction with the clinical eye of a research technologist in his laboratory, with no more feeling than the scalpel of a Dachau bone surgeon.

The mind was designed to keep body and soul (and mind) together. It was not intended to be so powerful as to block out the natural emotion of fear. If the mind can obliterate fear when there is every reason to feel fear then what can the mind not obliterate? Love? Compassion? The sight of blood? If you are not afraid when you should be afraid then you stand accused of stupidity. Your mind has sold you down a stream going nowhere.

In time that fall gave to me a fear, not a fear of broken bones or the impact after speed stops or even death, for you accept those possibilities in the act of commitment; no, not that, but a fear of a mind so delighted with its own capabilities and power that it has neglected the basics of doing what it is supposed to do, keeping body and soul and mind together.

My mind failed in allowing no fear to me as I was falling up a hill at 100 mph, but valuable lessons are locked up within your failures. I learned that my natural feelings are friends, not enemies to be crushed and avoided and suppressed by a mind gone mad with power. I learned that from my fall, but I didn't learn immediately.

CHAPTER TWELVE

Watching others do your work

I WAS EXTREMELY SORE for several days but I was crutching around the first night. Most of the men racers were on the town and I joined them. The next day was a rest for the men, a day for the women and juniors to run.

DiMarco wrote on my cast that night:

Al caro amico Dick con fraterno amicizio—
Luigi DiMarco
KL 173.493

And I wrote about him in my notes:

He is an honest man and a dedicated, courageous one. And it gives me a good feeling to have a man like that for my comrade and brother.

C.B. was really wound up. The timing was inconsistent and he felt constrained to run by the order the officials had set up. He also thought, as I did, the best times were to be found earlier, running on ice. C.B. had lost his record and he was not at home in Europe and it was a lot different than Portillo. My fall couldn't have helped his state of mind. He told me and all of Cervinia that he wanted to run on ice.

Miura had placed third with 169.014 and he had fallen, bounced and rolled, but both skis released and he walked away bruised but still in the game.

Journal, July 15, 1964:

The worst of recent days. I fell at 166 kph and broke slightly my right leg...I tore a bunch of muscles along with it. I am in a cast to the knee but it will be cut off in a month. Nothing is changed because of this, and I am very lucky to make a mistake at that speed and come out of it so well.

DiMarco took the record away with 173.493. I am very happy for him. He deserves it more than any man in the world.

But there is something wrong with the timing here. It didn't work most of the day, and my time was first announced at 166 and then it came out in the results as 160. It felt above 160 by quite a bit, so I am going by the way it was announced. C.B. is angry at the discrepancies and the way everything is being run; he will try it Friday on the ice. Since he has gone 168 he may get the record back. I hope he does. The leg still hurts and I feel like hell now, so it is not the time to write about what it is to me.

Journal, July 16, 1964

The leg hurts today and my doctor is unhappy with me for not staying in bed. (I had gone drinking and dancing on my cast the pervious night.) He is probably right so far as the leg but I am not up to the depression that would be mine if I stayed down. I do not want to think too much or too hard just yet about this thing. It occurs to me that I went too far and was too greedy. I am not sorry, for I have proved to myself what I needed to know, and if this broken leg is the price of that awareness, well, it is a fair exchange.

My leg, however, hurts like hell and I fear the doctor will tell me that he told me so. Perhaps it is the cognac and pernod I drank last night in the good company of DiMarco, Nicole, Messner, the Contact Binding people, and Fulvia and her husband.

As I was writing this and admiring the Matterhorn the women and juniors were running on the Plateau Rosa. They had an astounding day. The women's record of 127.659 kph, set by Emanuela Spreafico of Italy in 1963, was broken by four competing women. Christl Staffner, long time Austrian team member, led with 143.027. Spreafico went 138.621 and Great Britain's Anna Asheshov had 138.461.

Every junior went faster than 130 kph and four went over 140. The best, Antonio Sperotti, went 142.743. The previous year the best junior time was 116.887.

The women's record had gone up by 16 kph, the junior's by 26. Technique and equipment and mental attitudes do not usually improve that much in just one year. It was evident that the condition of the track was unusually good.

The men went back to it on the 17th. Franco Rivetti had arranged for me to see a bone specialist in Torino so I could not watch the competition. I returned that afternoon from Torino much relieved in mind and leg to know the hard pain I'd been having was caused by torn muscles, which would mend, and a cast constructed too tightly, which had been replaced by one more comfortable. The boys had had a busy day and their results showed the track was noticeably improved. Four had gone faster than 170 kph and seven had bettered the best time of 1963. I intuited it then and later became convinced that 1964 was a watershed in the evolution of speed skiing, a year that opened up the potential of a unique and dangerous endeavor. Speed skiing would never be the same.

Results of the first ten, July 17, 1964

Luigi DiMarco, Italy	172.248
Yuichiro Miura, Japan	171.510
Roberto Gasperl, Italy	170.940
Ivo Mahlknecht, Italy	170.132
Bruno Alberti, Italy	169.811
Renzo Zandegiacomo, Italy	169.252
C.B. Vaughan, USA	168.855
Walter Mussner, Italy	167.597
Alfred Plangger, Austria	167.364
Edoardo Agreiter, Italy	167.208

Miura fell again but walked away. His body seemed made of rubber, his will of steel, his bindings of magic.

C.B. was not performing up to his own expectations. This great red haired American giant had his own, inimitable way of expressing his thoughts when he chose to express them, and he caused waves enough among the officials to have the starting time on the 18th, the last day, moved up two hours. He remembered Portillo, the ice, the record. The Italians argued that only he wanted to run before the track softened. C.B. responded that that was fine, all he wanted was the timing system to function and he would run alone. The rest could wait until mid-afternoon. He just wanted the track when and how he wanted it, early and hard.

C.B. got his way, but the game being what it is and the players how they are the others weren't going to let him have his way to himself. And so Mother Nature's snow chemistry and C.B.'s persuasive powers set the stage for the most remarkable day in all speed skiing history to that point. It was a magnificent, blue sky, windless day in the summertime Alps. White glaring snow and blue sky supported by the mountains. July 18, 1964.

I was situated on the porch of the Plateau Rosa restaurant, three fourths of a mile from the track, with a head-on view of the run from a slightly higher elevation than the bottom. I could watch each racer's run from the start until he disappeared in the transition. I had a good pair of binoculars and the Italian Dogana (Border Guard) provided me with earphones so I could know the times. I remember intense expectation for I knew the track would be exceedingly fast.

While waiting for the first racer I jotted in my journal:

Miura fell at 169 on the day I fell. Yesterday he fell at 171. His bindings came off and he was not hurt either time. Yesterday he said to Nicole, "I hope I don't fall tomorrow. I don't like to fall like that."

Of such things are (were) Kamikaze pilots made.

The first racer was C.B. Even through the binoculars I knew before he was halfway down that an extremely fast run was happening. It was happening to C.B. while I watched and in the blink of a mental eye I realized Ron Funk's feelings ten months earlier. In Portillo I could not know what it is to see another man do the work you know is yours to do. To watch another man at your work is a hard lesson. (Journal: *It hurts more than I thought it could to watch the others doing my work.*) It is a feeling worse than when your love has been untrue. It is more like when you have been untrue. It is like that and it is bad. It is the end of creation. I realized all of that before C.B. stormed into the transition, and I was filled with a feeling explainable only by analogy.

C.B. never came out of the transition. He had fallen. While this was sinking in his time was announced. C.B. had tied DiMarco's record of 173.493. For the second time in a year Vaughan co-held the world speed record, but this time he fell. Before there was time to be worried for him the earphones informed me that C.B. was up and alright. He was reported to be surly and bruised and his racing tights were shredded, but he was on his way up for another run. That was the fastest an American traveled on skis as well as the fastest anyone fell off of them for a few years.

C.B.'s triumph was short. Alberti came and set a new record of 174.165. DiMarco, the master, put everything he had, which included a master's dedication, into his run and it was a new record of 174.757. No one could go any faster and did not for a few years.

While no more records fell the rest of the day was exciting. C.B. tried again a few times but never got above 170. Edoardo Agreiter, who once held the record, fell at 173.326 and broke his arm and dislocated his shoulder. Miura's hopes were in vain. He was blown over on his back before he got out of the trap but still managed 172.084. He walked away once again, but this time he walked more slowly.

When the day was over eleven men had traveled more than 170 kph and thirteen had broken the previous year's record. Until that week only C.B. and I had been over 170 kph.

Final results of first fifteen, July 13—18, 1964

Luigi DiMarco, Italy	174.757
Bruno Alberti, Italy	174.165
C.B. Vaughan, USA	173.493
Edoardo Agreiter, Italy	173.326
Ivo Mahlknecht, Italy	172.496
Kalevi Hakkinen, Finland	172.413

Yuichiro Miura, Japan	172.084
Heini Messner, Austria	171.265
Walter Mussner, Italy	171.102
Roberto Gasperl, Italy	170.940
Gildo Siorpaes, Italy	170.697
Felice De Nicolo, Italy	169.971
Renzo Zandegiacomo, Italy	169.411
Bruno De Zordo, Italy	169.411
Alfred Plangger, Austria	167.364

There was nothing to unwind from but I felt the way a man feels when he has watched others at his work. At the award ceremonies all the racers who had gone faster than 160 kph were given blue Lanciato sweaters and certificates of their speed. It was a happy affair and I was glad to have my sweater and to be among good comrades. I was happy and proud for Luigi, Bruno, C.B. and the others. They had created a fine day for themselves and had accomplished great things.

Naturally, it was a celebrative night but try as I could I did not feel my part in the merriment. I was a competitor and had violated a principle of the competitive world: I had failed. I had not prepared myself and I had paid. I was unable to compete when it was time—that day. I was full of myself and of the seeds of dissatisfaction which would bring me back to Cervinia the next year, but I drank everything in sight and danced my cast to shreds as my part of the Saturday afternoon speed run.

Dorworth on the track in Cervinia

BOOK THREE

Cervinia Again 1965

"What disturbs the regular method of heaven, comes into collision with the nature of things, prevents the accomplishment of the mysterious (operation of) heaven, scatters the herds of animals, makes the birds all sing at night, is calamitous to vegetation, and disastrous to all insects;—all this is owing, I conceive, to the error of governing men."

Chuang Tzu

The hundred mph club in Cervinia
Dorworth third from left with leg in a cast

CHAPTER ONE

The expatriate

FOR A MAN IN A FOREIGN COUNTRY with $200, a broken leg, tender buttocks and a strong reluctance to return to his native country the first consideration is a means of support. Kalevi Hakkinen was driving to Finland and had room for a crippled rider, and his route took him through Kufstein, Austria, home of the Kneissl ski factory. Then he had to pass through Heidelberg, Germany where Doug Salter, an old friend from the University of Nevada, junior ski racing and many social and intellectual endeavors was a lieutenant with the U.S. Army. Doug had come to Cervinia, arriving in time to see the last, incredible day of competition, but the only performance he saw of mine was a dance on a broken leg. He told me I had a European headquarters in Heidelberg.

Kalevi and I left Cervinia and drove thirteen hours through Italy, over Brenner Pass and into Austria. It was a July Sunday and I couldn't see enough of people, villages, countryside, cars, roads, trees, lakes, cafes and inns. I was smitten with Europe. We found ourselves behind a young Italian couple in a convertible. The man drove competitively and the girl had her arm around his neck, clearly her man's woman. We followed closely and competitively for several miles and the man laughed when we stayed with him through a hard section of the road. The girl laughed and waved. The inspired Kalevi coaxed his Porsche and we passed the couple coming out of a turn. The girl blew us a kiss and they both laughed and the girl was very pretty. In America the same situation would have produced set jaws rather than laughter, determination instead of inspiration, a curse and a raised middle finger in place of a wave and a kiss to help us on our journey. When we got to the Kneissl Hotel in Kufstein I was tired and ready to settle my bruised body into the puffy Austrian comforters. I was depressed by the leg and because I had to see the others run, but I went to sleep remembering a pretty girl who waved and blew a kiss and her man who laughed about it.

We waited most of the day to see Franz Kneissl, head of one of the largest ski companies of the time. When we finally got to see him we talked for four hours. Franz was powerfully active, intelligent and with a fine sense of humor, always a good clue to a man's character and quickness of mind. He wanted to know everything about speed skiing and other things—how it felt to fall at 100 mph, how his skis worked and how to make them better, what made Luigi the best, if I thought Barry Goldwater could be elected president (I met few Europeans who weren't horrified at the possibility), who would be the best American ski racer the next year, what kind of place was Portillo for the 1966 FIS World championships, but most of all Kneissl was interested in people. When Kalevi and I left I felt we could have easily talked for four hours more, and I had a job in Kufstein with Kneissl as soon as my leg healed.

. . . .

Heidelberg, the city of Sigmund Romberg, memories of the voice of Mario Lanza and "The Student Prince," impressions of Mark Twain and Somerset Maugham. Heidelberg is an ancient city full of cultural and historical significance which saved it from being bombed by the allies in World War II. Few experiences are more charming than being in a strange, beautiful city with friends who know that city and Doug and Charlotte Salter were friends and their home became my European headquarters. I explored the countryside, castles, cuisine and beer and met good people, both American and German. My knowledge of Europe gained scope and I began to exercise and write.

Journal, July 24, 1964:

A good morning of writing. It is harder and harder to be drawn between skiing and writing, but how tempting.

When I write as I have done today I am empty when it is over. I feel then like reading and exercising and drinking and making love.

It is dangerous to write in the first person. All writing is dangerous. The better you write the closer you get to the truth of yourself, and the truth is dangerous and terrible for each man because he must face it alone, and writers are the loneliest people. It is knowing yourself through risk and skill. The better you are the further you go, the further you go the higher the risk, and the more you know the more you reveal yourself. That is the most dangerous.

We investigated Heidelberg at night. My cast and crutches were an easy conversation piece and I soon became a curiosity among Heidelberg night people. Nothing intrigues a German easier than a man who lives close to physical pain, injury or death. Nighttime Heidelberg also revealed that 50,000 military Americans lived in the area.

Soon, it was time to move on to Paris, and I had a solid background of Impressionist art history, Hemingway, Gertrude Stein, Scott Fitzgerald, Balzac, Baudelaire, Henry Miller, Victor Hugo and Edith Piaf.

Before leaving, one German friend, a Hitler Youth leader decorated for gallantry in Italy, told me his version of the difference between German and French: "The French work to live; the German lives to work."

Another German friend who had been captured in the war by the French while still a teenager told me, "You Americans talk about how bad it was in German concentration camps. That's right, I'm sure it was bad. Germans can be cruel. But, let me tell you, to be a German in a French concentration camp is no fun. The Germans are precise and organized in their cruelties, but the French are more imaginative." That same German who carried a valid Argentine passport at all times and who many years later died an old man in Argentina, also told me that Germans like to make war and that the next time that happened he was going to South America. He believed the only way to avoid war is not to fight in them and he decided not to make war, ever again, and I believed him and agreed with him.

Armed with my expanding knowledge of Europe and Europeans, I progressed to France.

Paris is an experience first, a city second, and the first time in Paris is esoteric. I am not a city person but if I were Paris would be the city. I had the good fortune to have a Paris friend with an apartment, a car, a lifelong knowledge of Paris, a sense of humor, intelligence, a flaming desire to please me and my total enthusiasm. I called her 'Mon Cherie' only at first out of ignorance.

I removed my cast a bit too early and limped badly, as if walking on egg shells, but walking. I was happy in Paris. The speed run depression had vanished and I fell into a scheduled, productive existence.

We rose early and I wrote until midday. Then lunch and wine and museums or sight seeing or shopping. I tried to walk ten blocks a day and afterwards my leg was sore and I would rest in a sidewalk café with white wine or pernod, jotting in my notebooks, reading the newspaper and watching the people in the world's greatest city. Cherie had lived a very different life than the one I knew and we talked for hours in Paris sidewalk cafes about those differences and who we were because of them.

My favorite haunt was in impressionist gallery near the Louvre.

Journal, August 5, 1964:

I walked into a room today and the first thing I saw was my favorite Van Gogh. I could not believe the effect it had on me. The painting is Van Gogh's self-portrait in blue, his last self-portrait, I think. Certainly his best, one of the best I have ever seen. The most powerful.

It was like looking at a good print while stoned. I couldn't move from it and I finally left because I had to. But I came back. All the reading I have done on Van Gogh and all the prints I have studied taught me very little about the man. I learned more in 45 minutes in front of that painting about Van Gogh, his work, his tragedy and love, than I learned during the months it took to read three volumes of his letters.

If a person had that portrait on the wall of his dining room or bedroom he would go mad in six months. Mad with understanding and feeling and sorrow and love. And the mad man would be compelled to action, be it murder or work, drink and fight or heroin and flight.

Nothing I have seen has been like that. The closest I have experienced to what happened before that painting is being stoned.

Afterwards I did not want to see more. Not even the beautiful Renoirs in the next room, maybe especially the beautiful Renoirs.

I began to remember that my naked, unhindered, unclouded eye and mind will always perceive the truth if I let them.

An American among Frenchmen for the first time will view his country, his countrymen and himself in a different perspective than ever before. During this time a couple of Vietnamese sampans were said to have assaulted an American destroyer in the Gulf of Tonkin, providing the excuse for events too well known to repeat here. In Paris, my friends said the Gulf of Tonkin incident was reminiscent of Poland's invasion of Germany in 1938. And three American boys, civil rights activists of different colors, were found buried in a Mississippi dam. I knew a member of France's Communist Party and the USA was her least favorite country, though she was both charming and gracious with me. We had serious, heavy talks about the history, economic motivations and worth of my country, and the United States in Viet Nam and the hidden graves of some American boys in Mississippi were difficult points to debate with a French Communist in August 1964. They have not since become easier.

Gertrude Stein quoted Pablo Picasso saying, "Ils ne sont pas des hommes, ils ne sont pas des femmes, ils sont des Américains."

My notes refer to that quote:

It seems appropriate for Miss Stein, who appeared to have no sex but who was very much American, to quote that from a modern man who is very much a man and her good friend. Also, I think it more true now than when Picasso said it.

Journal, August 12, 1964:

Paris is full of Americans. I have seen them walk down rows of Gauguins, Lautrecs, Van Goghs, Cezannes, Monets, Seurats, Redons, etc., and aim their eyes at each painting for 3 to 5 seconds, 10 if they are interested. Three of them are in this café; the father is loud, the daughter vulgar, and the mother eats potato chips and talks about what she bought in Rome. I am sitting in a corner, writing, watching, trying to order vin blanc in my best Italian or Spanish accent.

It is a hell of a note to feel like that about your countrymen.

I was learning, however, that there were several manifestations of the same malady.

Journal, August 13, 1964:

Bud Powell is in town. He is a real piano player as Tatum, Peterson, Wilson and Mel Powell are piano players. Yet Bud Powell is almost totally unknown. Only the jazz student and the unusually appreciative know who he is or what, or, most important, how well he plays piano. I am sure Powell has not a good life. A fake like Al Hirt makes more money than he can spend, and in certain circles is considered a great jazz musician.

There is a relationship, springing from man's relationship with himself, between the comparison of Gertrude Stein with journalism and the unrecognition of Bud Powell and the idolatry of Al Hirt; a link exists between those and what causes war and why men beat other men to death because of their, the dead ones usually, color or beliefs.

Plato himself verifies this:

"Music and rhythm find their way into the secret places of the soul."

The world ignores Bud Powell and glorifies Al Hirt. That is not a pretty comment on the condition of the human soul.

Paris gave to me a beginning to the hard knowledge of the interconnectedness of all life, the continuing effect of the smallest action, the mushrooming destruction that grown from the smallest lie and the first dishonesty, everyman's innate responsibility to the universe.

Journal, August 15, 1964:

Man and truth. What a difficult match.

Besides their incompatibility, there is the further difficulty that man is so many things and truth also is many things. The exception is when the truth and the man are same. For instance: Art is truth and Picasso is an artist. Luckily, he is also a genius.

The truth of Bud Werner was ski racing. He knew his truth and he lived it, and Werner was a great man.

It is dangerous to find truth in athletics because almost always you out-live your truth, and the rest is a lie, at best a half-hidden truth.

The inward reality is the real truth of man. The outward reality is a product of fear, cowardliness, weakness and man's oppression of himself. The Inquisition was an outward reality and so is war. Spelling and geography are outward realities. Popularity is an outward reality. Death is an out-ward reality. Living is only real inside. There is just one reality for each man and that one is inside, and the man who communicates his reality— through art, through sports, through the way he builds a building or teaches a second grade class—is a lucky man. He is useful in the universe.

They who live by the inward reality are forever children, often lonely and sad, even tragic, but sometimes fulfilled, happy, beautiful and success-ful, even on the surface. If they are Picasso and Werner they are admired, respected and honored. Most are not and that is the price of knowledge of their own inward reality.

I am sick today when I think of the warping of values and ideas and of the pain inflicted on young minds and spirits by such as Finch and Rosaschi (two administrators during my school days) in the name of the outward reality. I remember the times I was forced to talk to those two. Even then I knew their stupidity and righteousness and the narrowness of their lives.

Yet, there is no answer. For someone warped Finch and Rosaschi a long time ago. They believe a principle is more worthy than a human, of more value than the humanity that principle supposedly benefits. That is not true; it is the perverse thinking of the outward reality; and there is nothing to be done for them. The hope is in the present and future, they are of the past.

And I am sick because the Finchs and Rosaschis control much of the present and therefore much of the future.

It is very sad.

Arles. I wanted to see another part of France and chose from my own inexperience. Van Gogh and Gauguin had lived in Arles and I wanted both to see why and to connect in some small way with those two great artists. I went to Arles.

I wandered the city of Van Gogh scenes and explored the old Roman ruins. I worked my imperfectly healed leg into a throbbing pain by long walks in the countryside outside Arles.

Journal, August 19, 1964:

The walk today was not a waste. The exercise I need and I am not sorry. The countryside is amazing. It looks like Van Gogh painted it. The country was here long before Van Gogh and it is still here and he is not. While I would be impressed by the scenery and rich land without knowing Van Gogh, I would not have recognized its beauty, life, or significance without his paintings. Van Gogh gave this landscape meaning for me. That suggests a great deal of what is an artist and where lies his place in this world. I have often thought that only some people have God in them, if there is a God, and if there is a God part of him was in Van Gogh.

Marseilles. One of Europe's oldest seaports. Rich. Wild. Open. Clear, shimmering air. Colorful and warm and full of movement. Marseilles displays some vital force of human existence that does not surface everywhere. Marseille is a Matisse in motion.

I had a strong personal contact with a group of French Algerians met in an Algerian bar. The climate of Marseilles is like that of Algeria, and when DeGaulle gave Algeria back to the Algerians many French Algerians moved to Marseilles. They felt DeGaulle had betrayed them. The only thing they hated more than DeGaulle were "those fucking niggers," which was the only English vocabulary of the bar owner referring to native Algerians. Those French Algerians in the bar all had white skin, were interesting and enjoyable drinking partners and conversationalists, and liked me because I was an American. Every newspaper in the world, they told me, said every day that Americans do not like "those fucking niggers." When I told them that all Americans were not the same I knew I did not speak for the majority and I was not proud of them or of my country, and I also knew my new French Algerian friends viewed my protestations with skepticism. And I could not blame them

St. Tropez. Play yard of the Paris rich, gathering spot of the jaded, the bizarre and the social freaks of Europe. I was completely comfortable and engaged in St. Tropez, a village and bay in the south of the Cote d'Azur on the Mediterranean Sea. The Allies landed there once, Winston Churchill on hand to watch. Cherie came from Paris and the weather was perfect for my first beach time in three years. The leg was sore but I was able to water ski on the other one. I started to regularly exercise my body and it was wonderful to think and live in physical terms again.

Journal, August 25, 1964:

My physical condition in disgusting. I do not like myself. Yesterday I had two turns on the water ski and swam a great deal. Today I am stiff beneath the burned skin. I hate to be like this. It fills me with disgust but it is excellent impetus to begin training.

Relativity. The people here think I'm the best water skier around, they have never seen a better one. They think I am good and I am not, though not so poor as they. They are impressed because their skiing standards are lower than mine. Mine, in turn, are lower than Ni Orsi's or Warren Weatherall's. Even among champions like that standards are relative, though more difficult to see.

Wolfgang Bartels (Bronze medal winner in the Olympic downhill) has had a serious car accident. He has the makings of a great one and I hope his skiing is not ended or impaired (His racing career was finished.) This has been a difficult year on skiers—Deaver, Werner, Henneberger, Bozon, and though they were not great skiers Barnes and Lyder were enthusiastic ones. I think the Gods are angry. There is no rationalization or happiness or reason to be made out of such things. One can only suppose Zeus has lost a few girls to skiers. That is no reason to believe in the existence of Zeus and the rest, but as good as supposing anything else.

And I knew a man in St. Tropez whose career had been in the French military. He carried some evil looking scars on his body (and, one assumes, his psyche) from Viet Nam in 1954 and Algeria somewhat later. Those scars and his membership in a prominent French family kept him from a stiff jail sentence when he chose to oppose DeGaulle returning Algeria to Algerians. He was barred for life from military and political activities and sometimes there was an acrid tone to his talk. One morning I was struggling with a French newspaper article about Viet Nam, but my knowledge of French was inadequate to the task. "Hey, Philippe," I asked, "What are the Americans doing in Viet Nam? "

"The same as us ten years ago," he answered curtly, without glancing at the newspaper. He was silent and angry and there was nothing more to be said.

Return to Heidelberg. The same beautiful, German city burdened with 50,000 American soldiers away from home. I had a few good days there before my friend Doug Salter gave me a ride to Kufstein. Time, once again, to settle in.

CHAPTER TWO

A life of discipline in Kufstein

KUFSTEIN. IN THE INN VALLEY just across the border from Germany. Hitler and Mussolini met there on September 28, 1939 when Austria was part of the Third Reich. It is a quiet village with mountains and forests rising from both sides of the valley. The Kneissl factory was the biggest industry in this Tyrol town halfway between Innsbruck and Munich, though much of the economy was fueled by Munich tourists.

I didn't know five German words when I arrived and fell into a solitary existence with thoughts my closest company, and I had a head full of a first exposure to Europe for companionship. Time to get my body back in shape. I felt like an overweight pro reporting to spring training.

I found a room with a family in their home. It was tiny, immaculate, on the edge of the village against a hill and perfect for my needs. I was nearly broke and the job with Kneissl paid the equivalent of U.S. $80 a month. I organized my existence with minimum financial expenditure and resorted to discipline, the strongest and most reliable of friends to those who know him.

My job was menial, difficult in the beginning because I had to stand for nine hours a day. I worked in a basement corner of the factory with five Austrians. We were responsible for removing and replacing ruined edges, tip guards and tail plates on skis brought back for repair.

I practiced German on my fellow workers but German is difficult. Most of my work mates spent their lives working at repetitious tasks, yet they were happy, intelligent people who accepted and looked forward to their daily toil. I admired their acceptance which I did not share. The sleek, fine lines and craftsmanship of any ski of any brand reminds me of my proud, cheerful co-workers in the basement of that factory. Today, when I see skis selling in the United States for $1,000 a pair I remember, and it shames and troubles me to remember that most of the people who made that ski cannot afford to ski.

My schedule was rigid, productive in its way.

5:30 a.m. Rise, wash, dress and read.

6:15 a.m. The Frau brought breakfast—Two cups of coffee, five pieces of bread, butter and jam. I drank one cup and ate three pieces of bread with all the jam. Butter the other pieces and wrap them in paper. Brush teeth. Drink the other cup of coffee to have the taste accompany me to work. Continue reading until time to leave.

6:40 a.m. Walk to the factory. Stop in a shop along the way to buy a piece of cheese or salami and an apple which, along with the bread saved from breakfast, was the mid-day meal.

7 a.m. Work.

12 noon. Lunch hour. Usually I sat outside, ate, and read, even when it was cold. Only when it rained did I stay inside, for factory air deflates consciousness.

1 p.m. Work.

5 p.m. End of work. Walk home, change clothes, and go into the hills for my workout which was brutal in the beginning, the most difficult time I'd had getting into shape. I no longer had the intense motivation of other times, but I ran for more than an hour, did a few calisthenics and paid close attention to my physical state. The mountains around Kufstein are honey-combed with trails and roads. To most Europeans I knew, walking is not just a means of getting from one place to another, but, rather, is a function, a pleasure, a healthy part of life and a communion with nature. There are walking trails on every mountain, in every woods, and to the extent that running is a pleasure (an individual measure) those trails were a pleasure to run upon.

For the first two weeks my leg hurt constantly and I was not secure while running. I chose each step with care. I dreaded those workout for their pain and for the possibility of further injury, but I had decided to race in Europe that winter and I had learned about not being prepared. Eventually the leg and the rest of the body came around. The soreness left the leg. The suety layer under the skin left my body. Instead of dreading the daily workouts I (borrowing from the Beattie vernacular of the day) 'attacked' the walking trails of the Tyrolean Alps. After a month I was not as strong as I needed, but I knew I would be. There was no doubt in my mind nor reluctance in my body.

Near the end of every workout I stopped on a bluff above the Kufstein glider field. Gliders fascinate me and I always finished my runs remembering huge, silent, bird-like machines cutting through the air like a slow-motion sword on an eternal sweep.

7:00 p.m. Return to the Kneissl factory to shower and shave. I had to get special permission to shower after hours and on weekends at the factory, but it would have cost 10 schillings (nearly 50 cents) for a single shower where I lived. That was impossible on my salary and it seemed intolerable to live without free access to a shower. I had gone few days in my life without bath or shower in hot water, and I was offended by my co-workers surprise when I insisted on showering each day. They laughed at my strange custom but were kind enough to help me arrange my showers in the factory. It didn't occur to me that anyone might take offense at my obvious surprise and condescension at their practice of showering but once a week, sometimes less. I wondered how they tolerated such a 'dirty' existence. Now I wonder that they who accepted life in a manner that any American could learn from, could tolerate such a naïve, snobbish American. Only twice did I see another worker use the showers. That seemed illogical to me and I was so American that I was not about to investigate any other logic than my own.

7:30 p.m. The hot meal of the day. I learned which Kufstein restaurants and items on the menu matched my budget and taste, and I ate this meal in a different restaurant each night. For a dollar I could get a glass of beer, a bowl of soup, an omelet and two rolls with butter. That was a few years before I became a vegetarian but it would have been a good time to start. I seldom ate meat, its price far exceeding its nutritive value as well as my finances. Sometimes I'd have a coffee after dinner to draw out this most pleasurable part of the day. My German never progressed to the point of casual conversation with strangers, so I watched people, jotted in my journal and analyzed loneliness, my closest companion.

After dinner I walked through the streets of Kufstein, looking in store windows, exploring new streets, watching the river and wondering about the lives behind the lighted windows in the Tyrol houses I didn't know. Eventually, depending on mood, I went to my room to read until I fell asleep,

That was my Monday through Friday work day.

On weekends I slept late, read, wrote, bought things I needed in town, read Time, the Herald Tribune or struggled with Le Monde. In the afternoons I went into the mountains for a four or five hour work-out. Those long workouts were my favorite times. I had never known such isolation among people as I did in Kufstein, and being alone in beautiful mountains was a more understandable and bearable form of solitude. And hard physical exertion can be the release of a multitude of pressures, the expiation of several sins.

There were breaks in my schedule and tone. Heini Messner and Kalevi showed up one day and I took them on my workout route in the mountains. DiMarco came by the factory one day and left after an hour. Once an American came by to buy rebuilt skis. He spoke no German and I was called from my work bench to help him. He was astounded to find an American at the Kneissl factory and he had a thousand questions. He was nearly ecstatic the discover I was a fellow Sigma Nu and when he gave me the secret handshake I was so surprised that I laughed and hurt his feelings. It was unreal, so far away, my membership in a brotherhood that excluded slaves and the descendants of slaves. I apologized for laughter, but it had been a long time since I'd done any secret handshaking.

A girl from Nevada was living in Madrid and she came to visit. We had once been close but had not seen each other in more than two years and we met again as strangers. We had a pleasant few days but when she left we both knew there was nothing left for us.

Cherie came from Paris and we explored the countryside together. She was remarkable and we enjoyed each other's company, but we had very different paths in life and when she left I never saw her again.

One early October Saturday my long run in the hills ground to a stop and I was overcome with the sameness of every day. On a sudden inspiration I raced back to town, cleaned up, dug into my savings and took the first train to Munich where Oktoberfest was in full swing. Unlike anything else in the universe, Oktoberfest consists of five or six circus tents, each advertising and serving the wares of a Munich brewery. Mugs of beer and roast chicken. In each tent were five to ten thousand people, sitting, standing, banging beer mugs in time and singing German songs to 30 piece oompah bands on podiums in the center of the tents.

I went to Oktoberfest to quell the restlessness of regimen. In that I failed, but I learned something I never understood before. To be in a tent with 10,000 singing, mostly drunk Germans, all keeping time to the biggest Oompah band there is in the same, heavy, simple rhythm is a powerful experience. For the first time I understood, viscerally, intuitively understood an individual giving his individuality to the mass. The German does not clap to keep time, he pounds, and his rhythm is the tempo of the march. I drank beer, ate chicken with my hands, sang and banged my mug in cadence with the march. I realized that the right piper, playing the just right tune on a silver, magical flute could enter on that rhythm and lead the entire tent—all Oktoberfest, the city of Munich, Germany itself along any path he chose. And the piper's march so often leads to destruction.

I returned to Kufstein without sleep at 8 a.m. astonishing my landlady, Frau Lucke, by the uncharacteristic break in my schedule. I wrote in my journal that afternoon:

Oktoberfest. It could only be in Germany. Only the German people could achieve Oktoberfest. In those huge tents, crammed with eating, singing, drinking people, one could see how Hitler did what he did, and one could see why he was allowed to do it. It may be unfair to draw a parallel between Hitler and Oktoberfest—the Germans have had so many parallels drawn between Hitler and almost everything—but only in Germany could Hitler have been and only Germany could create Oktoberfest, and for much the same reason. In Germany there truly is such a thing as national character.

And the girl with the beautiful black hair and wild cat eyes saved her money and showed up in Kufstein in mid-October. It had been four months and we had to learn to be together again. We did, but it no more than started to be good when, once again, it was time to move on. I had decided that I had one more year of racing left in me and that year would be in Europe.

CHAPTER THREE

Thrills, spills, and UFOs

A RACER WHO HAS NOT COMPETED IN EUROPE has missed a great part of what it is to ski race. Listing the great European champions is not necessary, but it is useful to recognize that in the 1960s a hundred skiers in Europe were good enough to make the national team of the United States at any given time. Under and because of Bob Beattie this situation improved and continues to improve, but the point is not the improvement of Americans but, rather, the superiority of Europeans at that time in matters of skiing. The European downhills are faster, longer and tougher than those in America. The classic courses in Chamonix, Wengen, Kitzbuehl, Cortina, Lenzerheide, St. Anton, Megeve and Sestriere bred a different attitude towards racing than was found in America. There was a huge economic and social advantage for a European to be a member of his or her country's national team. In the U.S. even the very best racers were hard pressed to continue racing past the age of 23 or 24 and few did, though that has changed for a few elite racers now. Basically, the difference between a European and American ski racer of the '60s was that disparity between the amateur and professional in any endeavor. The Neanderthal, class conscious athletic ideas of Avery Brundidge prevailed in America, while Europe took a more practical perspective of athletics, athletes and sportsmanship.

I wanted to experience European racing. I would not startle the skiing world with results of my old dreams but I would get by, and I could learn a few things worth passing on when it came my time.

In 1963 I applied to the USSA for a Class A International License which they more or less had to give me because I had finished in the first ten in the National Championships. 1964 was different and I had no illusions about how I was regarded in official U.S. skiing circles. It was not possible to enter a major race in Europe without that license and I applied for a credential I was not sure would be issued. A few weeks later it arrived with a letter wishing me the best and hoping that my injuries of July had healed. That letter was the first crack in my solid cynicism about the USSA, or at least my relationship to and part of it, and it was the first relief from several years of U.S. skiing paranoia. I was even a little warmed.

A trace of karmic awareness which I called superstition was entwined with my thoughts.

Journal, November 3, 1964:

And Zimmerman has had a wreck and will be out of action. Zeus is still not finished with the skiers. From what I know of Egon, Zeus has more reason to be angry with him than with the others he has picked on lately.

And tomorrow is election day in America. May Johnson never have had any affairs with Zeus' girls.

Apparently he had, even though he won the election

. . . .

In early November I quit my job, packed and had a farewell talk with Franz Kneissl. Of it I wrote:

Kneissl laughed and laughed when I told him I have no home base in Europe and am a traveling man. The Austrian is bound to his home; his morals, virtues and chief pleasures are those of the home. Not to have a home makes him laugh, I do not know from humor, strangeness or sadness. Kneissl is treating me well and with a little luck, a few good races and a ski lesson or two maybe I'll make it the winter without missing any meals. Even 'home' is relative.

I returned to Cervinia where there was good snow and I knew a few people and got rates on lifts and room. My black-haired friend went to Germany to seek employment with the U.S. military.

Those first days of skiing were harder than the first workouts in Kufstein. The leg swelled at the break and my back was very sore at night. Apparently I had strained my back in July's fall but it only told me about it when I skied hard. I pushed hard but each night I hurt and wondered if I'd ever get in skiing shape.

It came around.

Journal, November 21, 1964:

Two excellent days of slalom on perfect snow on the Ventina. There are no people. It is steeper than I usually use for slalom and some mental and technical weaknesses are brought out, but it is coming strong now and I feel wonderful. When I am skiing well or even beginning to, as I am now, I am at one with myself. That is the simplest way to explain it. I am myself and I am at one with myself.

Discipline breeds discipline and out of it comes a desire to work. Each day is easier because desire makes it seem easier. I set a goal each morning and the tiredness at the finish of the day is more reward than price.

One afternoon I returned from practice to find a telegram informing me that my aunt Llewellyn Gross was dead. Llewellyn, to whom I felt so close in spirit, who gave so much, one of Nevada's wealthiest women, died in her new, immense, expensive, blue Cadillac of carbon monoxide poisoning while driving alone from Reno to her Genoa ranch. So far as I know her death has never been explained and there is some reason to believe that The Mob, which was struggling with her husband Harvey, is a more likely culprit than a faulty muffler on a new Cadillac. Death is the other end of birth, a stage in the process of birth, growth, decay and transformation, but a man is never hardened to or completely understanding of some things. It had been a heavy year and a half and I walked the Cervinia streets late that night filled with grief and thoughts about what one does with this short life.

Journal, November 23, 1964:

The question of what I am going to do about the Lanciato is up before me. Quit, or go again? To be or not to be? One moment I am hot with excitement and hope of another record. The next I am cold with the knowledge of the actuality of speed. I also wonder if it matters anymore. One minute I think it matters terribly, the next I feel older than speed running.

There are several months left but I will have to decide. When the time comes I must commit or withdraw, and I must be perfectly sure. To choose wrong, either way, would be disastrous. Right now I have no idea what I will do, though I'm inclined to think I'll run.

A question, an inclination, but no answer.

Among my modes of survival that year was a periodic arrangement with the Heidelberg International Ski Club to teach skiing. This gave me extra money, free room and board while working and sporadic contact with fellow Americans from the military in Heidelberg. I would race and train a couple of weeks, teach skiing a week, and return to racing. A nice variety.

Thanksgiving with my Heidelberg friends at Kleine-Scheidegg at the base of the Eiger in Switzerland's Bernese Oberland which had the best snow in Europe that year at that time.

Then to Sportinia, Italy for the 'Cittadini' World Championships for skiers who live in a city not primarily a ski resort. The Italians, who have gambling but a more Catholic societal view of divorce than does my home town of Reno, agreed that Reno is not primarily a ski town and that I qualified as a Cittadini. There were really good skiers from Germany, Austria, Italy, France and Switzerland, many of them students with no desire to make their national team. Many of them skied better than most class A racers I knew in America. The depth of European skiing always amazed me. I had good start orders and I felt like racing. I fell in the giant slalom (won by a Frenchman named Serge Ramus who looked a great deal like Gaddis on skis). The first run of slalom I placed

7th with excessive caution. The second run I was more determined and I won by two seconds, not enough to make up for the first run but I finished 2nd in the race. It pleased me because I held my own against good Europeans and I knew what my mistakes had been. I enjoyed the game and results were secondary if important.

And then to Sestriere, Italy, near the French border. The Italian team was there as well as assorted individuals like myself, the Munich based Japanese skier Fukuhara, known as "Fuku," and the tiny Norwegian Johann Renander who had worked in the Kneissl factory. Sestriere had one of the best downhills in Europe and was my introduction to the form, and no matter how much skill or motivation a racer has or how much U.S. experience, first exposure to European downhill is a revelation. At least it was for me, an introduction to a different realm of skiing than I had known.

Journal, December 19, 1964:

Stiff and sore after a hard day of Sestriere downhill. I had one of the better falls of my life when I missed my pre-jump and landed in a flat going over 100 kph. My bindings came off and the big skis beat hell out of me. I admit to not feeling much like it but I went back up and ran a different line through the same section that put me back in confidence.

I fell in all the Sestriere races. My body was feeling a lifetime of injuries and falls and I was not completely recovered from the Lanciato. I stayed in Sestriere after the races to train and ski a few more days with the Italian ski team. The Italians were going to Selva Val Gardena where I was going to teach skiing during the Christmas holidays, and the Italian coach offered me a ride on their bus and the opportunity to forerun a series of Italian team races in Val Gardena.

This circumstance led to one of the strangest experiences of my life, one I do not pretend to understand or be able to explain, but which I am able to describe. We left Sestriere in the pre-dawn morning. The Italians were in a hotel a mile down the road from mine and our bus was to meet us at 4:30 a.m. I had taken my luggage there the night before and had only to walk the mile in the clear, December 14, 1964 air of the Italian Alps. It was a cold, starry morning. I was dressed warmly and was sensually happy to walk along a snowy road and to feel the cold and hear the snow squeak underfoot and to look at the stars in the dark sky.

Suddenly I noticed six bright, round objects in the sky. UFOs. Flying saucers. Space ships. Aberrations of the mind. God wishes in a Godless world. Whatever they are called or however they are perceived, I watched six of them for nearly ten minutes in the early morning of December 14, 1964 while walking down a road in Sestriere, Italy. They were white and moved in formation—two rows of three—but they did not move as one. They did not seem hostile and I was not afraid. They flew patterns that changed directions frequently and they moved with incredible speed. At one point they hovered above me. Finally, they flew off with great speed and disappeared. I continued my walk to the Italian team's hotel and rode the bus with them across Italy to Val Gardena.

My knowledge of neither the Italian language nor the mentalities of my Italian friends permitted me to discuss what I had just seen with them. That night in my hotel room in Val Gardena I noted the occurrence in my journal, and, with what to me is a strangeness at least as significant as seeing them in the first place, I forgot about it entirely by morning. I never remembered or thought about it again until a few years later when I re-read my notes of the time in the process of writing this book. Then I remembered the event perfectly, with a clarity and recall as startling as the original experience. I could hardly believe I had put it out of my mind so thoroughly. The valuable lesson for me is not so much that I watched for several minutes six of the mysterious, controversial UFOs, but that my mind is capable of completely blanking out the experience, the memory, the knowledge of what may be a key or at least a building block to a better understanding of the universe, or at least of ourselves.

The mind, too, has moments when courage is difficult, but courage is always available and is waiting for the call and opportunity to return.

In those days the downhill at Selva was short and ferocious. After training with the Italians I felt confident enough to decide that the only way to compete with them is through a total approach or enthusiasm and commitment. Letting, as they say, go.

Journal, December 16, 1964:

Today I was a hell of a downhiller, for awhile. When they picked me out of the woods Giorgio Mahlknecht kept murmuring "troppo forte, piano, piano," and now everyone is looking strangely at me and two of the racers call me "senza paura." Io non sono senza paura, ma e possible io sono senza intelligente. I was, as I said, a hell of a downhillers for a third of the course, and now my back and neck feel like they've just come off a torture rack. I can barely move despite a hot bath, and I have retired from skiing for the day. We'll see about tomorrow tomorrow, but right now I am not optimistic. Today, however, I was a hell of a downhiller for awhile.

My feet are sore from boots, my legs and hands from slalom poles, my lips from sun, my shoulder from a fall in slalom practice, my neck and back from being a hell of a downhiller for awhile, and my ego from Sestriere.

I sat around for a few days before attempting slalom. After my first attempt I noted:

I'm worried about my back. I can't ski at all without Zeus hitting me in the back with a Zeus sized baseball bat. I am also worried about becoming a hypochondriac. My only defense is that when it hurts too much to ski it hurts.

After that I watched downhill practice, took hot baths, and read. I saw two of the most spectacular skiing mistakes I've ever seen. Near the bottom of the Selva course was a jump off a road followed by a hard left hand turn into a gully and then the final straight schuss to the finish. The jump made it difficult to begin the turn correctly and racers were sometimes late and wide into the schuss. Now and then a racer was unable to make the turn at all, in which case he went straight up the other side of the gully to the top of a small ridge separating the first gully from a second one, and was lofted into space. He would then come down on the far side of the second gully or in its bottom. Racers were moving about 60 mph and tried very hard not to make mistakes.

Gildo Siorpaes, who went 170.697 in Cervinia, came off the jump sitting slightly back and was not even close to making the turn. He went up the bank and into the air completely out of control, but Siorpaes is big for a skier and very strong. He found his balance in mid-air and dropped from about 20 feet into the bottom of the second gully and didn't fall. Eventually he even got back to the course. It was a fine recovery.

Walter Mussner, who had such a strong facial resemblance to Bud Werner and who had gone 171.102 in Cervinia, flew too far off the jump, landed on one ski and rocketed up the side of the gully to the ridge. Just before reaching the top he began to fall and when he became airborne there was no sense of human control about the shot crow figure 30 or 40 feet above the snow. It was the most spectacular fall I had seen, and I thought of it often after I watched Walter fall again several months later. Walter wasn't seriously hurt but his face was cut and bruised and his neck and back were sprained. He was in bed in the same Pension and we visited and compared injuries and pains and talked about past and future Lanciatos. Mussner is mentioned in my notes as having "the most interesting line:"

Journal, December 18, 1964:

The snow is icy and difficult today. Some excellent falls and interesting lines. It is all very exciting. It has been a long time since I've just watched downhill; it is nearly as exciting as running. The crowd is going wild, taking particular delight in the better falls and more imaginative lines. When a downhill racer is in trouble it is amazing what the survival instinct will do for him. The most interesting line was just run by a racer in trouble. He wound up about 200 feet from the course after going off the ridge that separates the course from the Poma lift. I estimate his height—flying elevation— at 30 40 feet. He hasn't moved since he came down and he is surrounded by people. As Warren Miller would say, "And the crowd went wild." The poor bastard. This is educational enough that I think all racers should watch a downhill every now and then. It's fascinating. The next round of runs is due soon and the crowd is muttering expectantly. Crowds are wonderful. I must admit, no matter how much sympathy I have with the racer, I have the same expectation and emotion surpassing interest in the difficulties of the racers. Alas, I am of the crowd right now. I know better and I am not proud and it is one of the lesser human traits. It is the same in boxing and car racing and the rest. I am human like the rest of the crowd, but every time I sense a thrill at a racer's fall, or two boxers beating the crap out of each other, or a driver in the escape lane or upside down I feel guilt for the inhumanity of man which is in every man.

CHAPTER FOUR

Commitment is more than a decision

It was a fine Christmas at the Refugio Cir a few miles above Selva. I taught skiing and had a memorable holiday with the black haired one, the Salters and others from Heidelberg. I skied well enough to instruct but my back hurt constantly. One of my students said he could maneuver me into the American military hospital in Heidelberg to have it checked, and I returned to Heidelberg the day after Christmas.

Journal, December 26, 1964:
Life is good but my back isn't. It is good for skiing that there is also life. There is, as well, the Kilometro Lanciato which commits me to it almost as a natural course of things. Was all the rest designed to commit me to that one things so much against my nature? Am I, after all, only a proving grounds?

The military doctors said nothing was broken but my back was severely sprained. Two months of complete rest would help. It wasn't likely I'd take two months off, but to stop doing whatever caused pain was imperative. Some mornings just getting out of bed was very painful, but I was anxious to race. So, after a memorable New Year's Eve, during which Salter and I were involved in an altercation with a very drunk, belligerent and violent U.S. Army Captain and were rescued by the beautiful, black-haired one who bopped the Captain in the head with a full bottle of champagne which sent the fighting Captain to the hospital, I said goodbye to my Heidelberg friends including our lovely savior with sad eyes who was returning to the United States, and went to Wengen, Switzerland for the Lauberhorn.

The Lauberhorn downhill starts atop the Kleine Scheidigg T-Bar and finishes in Wengen, more than three miles below. The massive, impressive North Face of the Eiger is off the left shoulder when standing in the starting gate. It is a beautiful downhill and very long. Though I was far from physically or mentally at my best, I had a wonderful time on that course.

Journal, January 4, 1965

Early morning. Eating a day old sandwich for breakfast and waiting for the first train to Lauterbrunnen. I have forgotten my helmet in Heidelberg. And I have no parka, no wax kit, no file. I must be the most ill-equipped racer to ever be nervous about the Lauberhorn. I can't imagine forgetting my helmet. There were too many things on my mind when I left, which shows how simple a racer must keep his life in order to run good races. I can buy or borrow the helmet or wax but the rest can only be bought from myself, and there is no borrowing.

Journal, January 7, 1965:

Downhill is getting rough. Manninen and Minsch, both of the first seeding, are out with injuries, Minsch's serious. Two Germans are out also. There have been some terrible falls which I have avoided with luck and prudence. Today I was very confident. Had fun on the fast bumpy section at the bottom.

Journal, January 8, 1965:

I don't think I am able to commit myself to this race. I can't say if it is cowardice, concern for other things, lack of caring, or just the inability to commit myself in this tough a course. I do not feel competitive in the sense I have always tried to be a competitor. It may be that I should have come to Europe when I was 18.

I raced as expected, steady and slow, but I finished the downhill without falling. My slalom was poor because the slalom hill was artificially iced and I simply could not ski on ice. I was embarrassed to be there.

The next race was the Arlberg Kandahar in St. Anton, Austria. I got a ride there from Switzerland with Harvey Edwards, an expatriate American journalist and film maker living in Chamonix who covered Europe for Skiing Magazine. During the drive we had a fine conversation about Greece, living in Europe, writing as a craft, a piece he was writing about Francois Bonlieu and when he arrived in St. Anton he gave me a copy of "Zorba the Greek" by Nilos Kazantzakis. I was happy for the drive and the good company and to be in St. Anton, a lovely town and very famous in skiing. But the night I arrived I wrote in my journal:

I wish I were on a warm Pacific island with books, paper, pen and a native girl who said nothing because we spoke different languages. That way communication would be above board and we could smile and make love and not worry about the rest. One can live on bananas and coconut and sleep in a grass hut in the warm Pacific. It is cold in the Arlberg and when the races are over I am finished. I have 350 schillings, $20 and room and board paid up to Sunday. I feel the cold already.

Journal, January 13, 1965:

Today I had two runs, the first to warm up, the second to look at and practice the downhill. There were plans of more but about 1/3 the way down I threw my skis sideways on a flat in order to stop. I was slowed to about 15 mph when I caught both outside edges. I had a fall so quick and hard it was over before I knew I'd fallen. The effect was like playing snap the whip with my back.

I could barely ski the rest of the way down. I had to stop each time I hit a bump or turned hard, and I couldn't put myself in a tuck position.

I talked to Harvey, ate, came to my room in Haus Pepi Gabl, washed clothes and shaved. My back feels like a sprain under pressure. The realization of being finished as a ski racer has dawned. I am finished and I know it. This means a lot of things and can be put several ways. What it means to me and the way I put it (to myself) is that I don't have the strength of will anymore to sit out my injuries, get back in shape and try again another year. I don't have that anymore. I can't do it. That's what being finished means. What hurts more than my back is that I am finished without the sense of accomplishment that I somehow feel I should have. Maybe the latter is really what being finished means.

When any love ends the best way is to break clean. I will try to be strong and honest enough to do that. My plans are to stay in St. Anton, watch the AK and leave as a different kind of man in a different kind of world, doing different kinds of things.

I stayed in St. Anton with a back so sore that some days I had to crawl out of bed hands first before kneeling on the floor and raising myself to standing by holding on to the table. I took walks and saunas and read and wrote and explored St. Anton. I thought about what I wanted in life and what was best to do with myself. I had both grown as a person and hidden from aspects of society I didn't like through my immersion in ski racing, but I was sincerely concerned with what I should and should not be doing. I knew for sure that it was not ski racing. There were business opportunities in America but I am not a businessman or salesman, and I wanted to stay in Europe.

When there was only enough money for a train ticket and a little more I returned to my European headquarters in Heidelberg. My lovely friend had stayed instead of returning to America. Her presence was a lovely surprise but I was restless. After a week in Germany I borrowed some money and hitchhiked to Rome with Greg Salter, Doug's youngest brother. It was a good trip. We saw cities, works of art and architecture and geography I'd studied and was informed to see. After ten days of sleeping in barns, on the floors of good Samaritans and in cheap pensions, we made a 30 hour hitchhiking, train-riding push from Rome to Heidelberg. I decided to stand awhile. I was changing and grappling with the change and I returned to Heidelberg with an abundance of philosophical questions and a scarcity of practical answers.

Journal, February 2, 1965:

The tramp is running out of me, not because I object to the life or its hardships but because tramping produces the same loneliness and restlessness it used to relieve. This is the last time. I will always travel and wander but never again like this. I am not sorry to end it just as I am not sorry to have had it, but I am turning into a different man because I am ending it and, in the same context, because I have had it.

Changes. Is it for the good or is it failure? Only time will tell. I can see good and failure in what is happening to me. No one can add it all up until it is all over.

I cashed in my remaining link with the U.S., a plane ticket to New York, and found a job with a moving company earning DM 3.14 (about 80 cents) an hour. My employer, Horst Huttinger, best described as a sort of German Zorba, was a solid friend who provided me with a means to stay in Europe. The black haired one landed a secretary job paying American wages and military P-X privileges and we rented a giant one room loft in the Rohrbach section of Heidelberg.

One week I was destitute, depressed, physically damaged and without direction, and the next week I was employed, residing and creating magic with a beautiful girl in a great and ancient city, and living a standard higher than most people of any country.

But the embers of yesterday's fire still glowed.

Journal, February, 18, 1965:

A letter from Jan came. She said that my attitude of positiveness in Chile should have taught her a lesson about the way to attempt anything. She failed her foreign service exam because she convinced herself beforehand that she would fail. Perhaps I could learn a valuable lesson from an attitude I had in Chile a long time ago, many miles away, an attitude I must remember if I try another speed run. And I think I will try one more in Cervinia, possibly another in Portillo. There are good reasons for not going again but they are overshadowed by the manner of not quitting on a broken leg. The fact is I am not ready to quit, though I am finished competing.

None of that is sure. I am only thinking.

After my first day of work I wrote in my journal:

Now I must lead a scheduled, disciplined life until at least mid-summer. I must train, read, write, study and lift myself from the recent mental attitude. I must get my body in shape for the Lanciato, in case. I must get my mind and spirit in shape for when I go wandering again.

Journal, March 8, 1965:

I am a skier even when I am fat and out of shape and not on skis and far (in more than one respect) from the mountains. Next year I won't miss skiing as I have this time. I don't care what I have to do, next year I shall ski.

Don Brooks and Tammy Dix both made Beattie's team for Vail. That makes me feel good and it makes me feel very good about skiing. Both yesterday and the day before we ran slalom on the Konigstuhl. I was horrible and out of shape, but it was good for me and my back didn't hurt. As always when I come back to skiing I felt grand.

Germany in winter is like living under a rock. It is always cloudy and often it rains but the forests are green. In some respects, any scheduled existence is like living under a rock, but Heidelberg is a good city if one is to be in a city, and for the second year I settled into a happy time in a good place with the same good woman. I went to work at 6 or 7 a.m. and usually worked 10 hours. Most of the time I did office work, especially the English correspondence, but I also worked on the trucks as a mover of furniture and other things with which we clutter up our homes.

Most of the people we moved were American soldiers and their families, people whose life styles, aspirations, thoughts and justifications were in many ways quite different than my own. I learned more about the United States of America by moving a few American soldiers in and out of their German homes than I had learned in a lifetime of schooling and living in my country.

My country and what it was and was doing in the world took much of my thoughts that year. Most of my American friends were military people and none of them had satisfactory answers to my questions nor objective responses to my observations about their unsatisfactory answers to my questions. I thought I was the only American in the world who did not understand what my country was doing in Viet Nam. I wasn't, then or later, but that winter I looked closer than ever before at some of the basic values, ideals, ideas and practices that I had formed during my public school education. And everything I saw did not make me happy or instill confidence in my country, and a certainty grew out of an old suspicion—a great deal of my public school education had been a lie.

The naïve American is the most naïve of all because he takes for granted that he is the most civilized, or, in a more modern political vernacular, he takes for granted America's 'exceptionalism' which, of course, not to put too fine a point on it, is bullshit.

I thought about myself and what to do now that racing was over. By nature and habit I was unsuited for most of the possibilities open to me. The individual, solitary work of writing is how I wanted to earn my way in life, and I searched my ski racing career for mistakes to be avoided as a writer, lessons to be learned as a man.

Journal, March 9, 1965:

Off work early today and delighted for the time. To do what? Write, read, exercise; what else is there? Right now, nothing. Time will change and I with them and for now I must sit it out.

Today I have been full of what to do with myself. That is, I know I must commit myself to writing, but how? When? Where? What to do? I must have faith and keep with it and one day I will throw over all else, including convention, for it. Today I am full of the problem, its implications and practicalities, both moral and physical. I must learn my craft as a writer as I once learned to ski. I have the lessons of my skiing to go on and I will not make those same mistakes again.

Lesson #1: Do not turn down praise and acceptance if it comes, but do not seek them in any form. You write for yourself.

Lesson #2: Do not become bitter because things are not the way they are supposed to be. The fault is as much in thinking things are supposed to be a certain way as in who or whatever shows you that they are not. Happiness and justification lie in the writing and in the completion of the writing, not in what happens to it afterwards. You write for yourself.

Lesson #3: The one irrevocable truth is death. Death means bad luck, weakness, cowardice or a lack of time. Since death comes to all men and to all endeavors the greatest nobility is not found in morals or conventions, but in a man's insistence on his own free will in his life. A man writes for himself the same way a person is charitable for himself and the way a person is self-ish for himself. You write for yourself.

Lesson #4: Work like hell and watch the masters, but do not let them browbeat you. All masters are dangerous that way. Hemingway is the most dangerous.

Lesson #5: Work like hell and keep your private life out of the way of your work. That is impossible as perfection is impossible, but do it anyway.

Lesson #6: Two hours every day is better than fourteen hours one day a week.

Lesson #7: All creation comes from inspiration, and without discipline all inspiration is like the disconnected, split thoughts of a mind on pot.

Lesson #8: Ignore people, even your friends, maybe especially your friends. That is impossible but people are fools so do it anyway. As mentioned, you write for yourself.

Lesson #9: Never give up. It is the last endeavor there will be time for, and once it is begun it can never be abandoned. Death will give relief all too soon from the pain of attempt. It will help here if you never question too closely what meaning or value it has. Just do it.

Lesson #10: Women. Be careful! They can ruin everything good in a man and never be understood. They can rob you of your strength and will and power; and all censorship, be it women or government, has but one aim. Be careful of women if you want to create anything or do anything except make money for them. It is harder to ignore women than people but just as necessary. I have heard that a woman can be the most wonderful thing that can happen to a man, especially one whose loneliness is endeavor outside the accepted; but I have concluded, after serious study, that this is rumor, myth, sentimental dreaming or another facet of the Cinderella myth. Do not let your penis interfere with your pen or paint brush.

Time for exercise.

I went skiing in the Arlberg one March weekend. Of it I wrote:

I skied surprisingly well for my condition, far better than I expected. I felt the way I do when I ski right.

Skiing is a difficult talent to possess and even more difficult to maintain. A man who possesses a difficult talent cannot be said to truly possess anything, even himself.

A talent possesses everything and consumes everything and is everything. It pays for its selfishness with beauty and fulfillment and by putting people at one with themselves. The vengeance of a difficult, beauty giving, fulfilling talent spurned is more harsh a hundred than the most vengeful spurned woman. Its vengeance starts inside and works out, the opposite method from spurned women and much more destructive and cruel. I must be careful and get back to the mountains.

And I began serious workouts.

Journal, March 16, 1965:

Exercises yesterday:

40 pushups

50 leg raises

350 knee bends in tuck position

40 pushups

65 leg wheels

30 pushups

40 leg raises

100 toe raises

50 one legged knee bends on each leg

I have about decided that if I can get in shape I will run for speed. Once more? How little I knew when I finished the first time and said never again. Almost all depends on my physical condition.

I sit at my desk on a rainy Heidelberg afternoon, unable to work out, fat and out of shape, and thinking of going 100 mph on a pair of skis. Absurd!

Journal, March 18, 1965:

Yesterday I drove to Kaiserslautern with Rehberger. This quiet, formal little man told me war stories, chuckling like an impish schoolboy over some of them. He was on Rommel's staff in North Africa and he fought on the Russian front in the Tanks Corps. He told me stories of Rommel, the fighting in North Africa, and of POW life under the French in North Africa, the Americans all over the U.S. and the English in England. He was away from his home for nine years and says neither he not his 15 year old son will ever wear a military uniform of any country or government. It is all nonsense, he says. I would never have thought Rehberger had such a life. He was a Nazi and I wouldn't have thought that either. I need much education.

Workouts became my outlet for frustration. I ran in the hills behind Rohrbach and discovered a trail that went to Bammental, the tiny village where both my employer and friend, Horst Huttinger, and my old friend and sometimes running partner, Doug Salter, lived. The hills of Rohrbach and Bammental were heavily covered with trees, shrubs, ferns, grasses and brush, all usually wet and green and lovely. A large hill separates the two places and half the run was uphill. I timed my runs and kept to the same course. At first it took an hour and twenty minutes, but I worked that down to fifty five minutes. There were shorter runs closer to Rohrbach, the best of them I called "The Windmill" in honor of Don Quixote for the hundred yard uphill sprint in the center of it.

By April 9 my exercises included:

40 pushups

50 setups

550 knee bends in tuck position

40 pushups

50 leg wheels

125 toe raises in 3 positions

The Lanciato churned in my mind. I wrote a couple of friends in the States about the problem I was having with it to see what reflection they would cast. Both were negative.

Journal, April 19, 1965:

> *The Lanciato. Both Rod and Ray in their recent good letters expressed disapproval of my running another time. Rod because he didn't want me to hurt myself anymore. Ray because it takes too much (and offers too much risk) for what it gives or means to me anymore. It is easy to see their points. I have been hurt too often to relish more, but I know I am able to risk all if I think it worthwhile. Does it matter? Do I have anything to seek or prove, or am I only hanging on to another time? Questions I must answer. There must be a substance to them.*

Another question appeared in my life. I had been offered a job as a junior coach in the United states. It was just what I was capable of doing, the pay was enough to allow me to live the way I lived by working only six months a year, and it was enticing in other ways. But I was familiar with the parental syndrome and the Little League aspect of junior ski racing in America and was extremely hesitant about involving myself in such a scene. I liked Europe and wanted to stay, but I was working for DM 3.14 an hour and there was a job in California offering $5,000 in six months. I was determined to ski and the personal battle with greed was far from won.

May 1st is the world's Socialist holiday, the worker's day, and the workers of Europe recognize it as they do not in America. Over the May 1st weekend I took a skiing trip with one of my favorite people in a lifetime of knowing some very good ones—Rex Gribble, an expatriate American Heidelbergian since the early 1950s, not quite old enough to be my father but with enough years, experience and intuitive wisdom to have long before separated the wheat from the chaff of life. Rex's philosophy paraphrases Voltaire: "This is the best of all possible worlds because it's the only one there is;" shows traces of Ring Lardner: "Life is like a baseball player rounding third base, pumping for home, hat off and hair flying, cleats digging like mad, and home plate isn't there;" and reveals the soundest values and most solid respect and love for the game of life:

"I flew 107 combat fighter missions in the Pacific during World War II, and I never shot down a single enemy plane, and no enemy shot down me. And that's a lot better score than 20 to 1, my favor."

Rex and I skied in Stuben in the Arlberg, barely missing two avalanches that day, one of which blocked the road to Innsbruck and the Brenner, and were forced to detour through Germany in Rex's tiny car. It was engrossing and fun to talk about life with Rex and we drank beer and arrived in Selva to find a party with Salter and friends in fine spirits. We stayed up late, rose early and skied hard until early afternoon. Before leaving we stopped in a café for lunch. Carlo Senoner, who would become World Champion in slalom a year later, was there and it was good to see him. We talked about racing and the Lanciato and about our recoveries from old injuries, two old ski racers/speed skiers talking about life.

During the long ride back to Heidelberg I thought about the Lanciato and how all the questions and confusion and alternatives and doubts and pros and cons all boiled down, as everything in human life does, to a choice: yes or no.

Journal, May 5, 1965:

And I will. I am ready and it is a great relief not to be burdened with the weight of indecision. I feel wonderful about it.

Journal, May 6, 1965:

My main concern is physical conditioning and with that, at last, I am doing a good job. It is natural to do a good job at something. I will be ready for Cervinia.

It was important to maintain a positive attitude while looking to the future and taking care of the present. I constantly reminded myself of all I knew and of the necessity not to forget any of it, even for an instant.

Journal, May 10, 1965:

One must look forward. Looking back is like turning right at

Indianapolis, and even Vukovitch turned right once.

Choosing to run in Cervinia, saying yes to the choices within, rearranged my attitude and cleared my mind.

Journal, May 14, 1965:

Today is one of those fantastic spring days that cause young people to flunk out of school, fornicate in the grass, drink beer, lay in the sun and know deep within that the world is actually theirs. The kind of day that makes old people long so hard for their youth that they actually feel it is still theirs. The kind of day that solidifies my restlessness. A beautiful day in every sense.

My workouts were the hardest I had ever put myself through and I was really strong, having discovered a new approach, another dimension of how to play the game.

Journal, May 19, 1965:

In addition to my regular exercises I am doing something new. I put my ski boots and helmet and goggles on and hold my poles, and, studying both the good image of DiMarco and my own image in a full length mirror, I try to reach his position, perfect it

And then hold it for as long as possible. Until I began studying this picture, practicing this exercise (one of the most difficult I know) I did not realize the extent of what Luigi is doing, of how little I really know about speed skiing. At least the future of speed skiing. The future will be founded on what Luigi has done and very few (including the racers) realize what he has done and will do. The best way to discover it is to study closely a good picture of Luigi at high speeds, practice that position, and be strong enough to hold it going much faster than the photograph it was learned from.

Journal, May 24, 1965:

One has difficulty not agreeing with (James) Baldwin. It is so well put. The following smacks of Henry Miller in another key, a black one.

"Life is tragic simply because the earth turns and the sun inexorably rises and sets, and one day, for each of us, the sun will go down for the last, last time. Perhaps the whole root of our trouble, the human trouble, is that we will sacrifice all the beauty of our lives, will imprison ourselves in taboos, totems, crosses, blood sacrifices, steeples, mosques, races, armies, flags, nations, in order to deny the fact of death, which is the only fact we have. It seems to me that one ought to rejoice in the fact of death—ought to decide, indeed, to earn one's death by confronting with passion the conundrum of life. One is responsible to life: It is the small beacon in that terrifying darkness from which we came and to which we shall return. One must negotiate this passage as nobly as possible, for the sake of those who are coming after us. But white Americans do not believe in death, and this is why the darkness of my skin intimidates them."

I developed a special exercise to strengthen my ability to hold an extreme, low Lanciato position. To put my body in this position is was necessary to undo the top buckles of my boots. This decreased control but improved position, and hard application of this exercise increased the strength of my thighs greatly. At the proper time I was inexpressibly grateful for that strength.

Exercises, May 27, 1965:
>   Complete warm up exercises
>   40 pushups
>   50 setups
>   500 knee bends in tuck position
>   40 pushups
>   20 Ericson stomach exercises
>   80 leg wheels
>   40 pushups
>   60 leg raises
>   100 Lanciato exercises
>   20 Lanciato exercises after a rest
>   30 leg raises with ski boots on

140 toe raises in three positions
60 leg raises
110 Lanciato exercises
120 Lanciato exercises after a rest
30 leg raises with ski boots on
60 leg wheels

I needed help to compete in Cervinia and wrote Franz Kneissl to explain my position. He answered that whatever was necessary could be arranged, and I went to Kufstein to discuss it. Once again, Kneissl gave me more help that I ever received from my own country and I was both grateful and informed by his generosity. We discussed my ideas about skis for big speeds and I learned more about skis in a couple of hours with Franz than I knew from a lifetime of skiing. Special speed suits were necessary; it was no longer enough to have just skin tight clothing and suits of a special material were expensive. What we needed was made in Monza, Italy and Kneissl got it for me. And Egon would be in Cervinia a week before the races.

Then I went to Lech, Austria to see Martin Strolz. Martin, one of the world's best downhill racers in the mid-'50s, custom made some of the best boots of the time. We talked about his racing time in America and about Ralph Miller and Ron Funk and about the place of the Lanciato in skiing, and he made for me the boots I needed.

I returned to Heidelberg for the last period of preparation. I was completely committed.

CHAPTER FIVE

In love with living

THERE WOULD BE NO MORE COMPETITIVE SKIING after Cervinia and I approached my retirement like a wise, old fighter moving in on a talented, brash, new one. I was shedding a familiar and loved way of life for a different one while groping in the remembered knowledge that everything is a part of everyone.

Journal, June 1, 1965:

The hardest thing about taking risks is that one does not risk only himself. He is just one portion of the living he represents. For sure, the one who stands to lose the most, but there are others who do not risk, nor want to, who wish only to go through a happy life in peace, who might lose an amount too dear to measure in the loss of another.

Whatever a person does affects every person who loves him, even everyone who knows him. As soon as you make a friendship, fall in love, gain a respect, make an enemy, cause a baby to be born, as soon as your mother gives birth to you, you become a part of someone else and you do not walk alone.

At times one cannot feel but completely alone. Either painfully lonely or necessarily detached. Those are the times when he must be most aware of the people to whom he matters.

It is true that no man is an island. But sometimes a man is a drop of water flung off the crest of a wave, hanging in the unknown air above the seas he came from, a brief, instant star, falling back to nothingness in the great sea of life.

All of which is about myself and Cervinia. If I should have the bad luck and lack of time to kill myself, or even the worse luck with more time to cripple myself, it would for all intents mean the breaking and destruction of my good family. Not by itself, of course, but the proverbial last straw.

I must try. It is my last go at competitive skiing. But I must go with full awareness of the risks I take with me.

There is, I believe, a great deal gained by being aware. Awareness is an amoral form of honesty.

Exercises, June 3, 1965

> 40 pushups
> 50 setups
> 600 knee bends in tuck, heels raised
> 40 pushups
> 20 Ericson stomach exercises
> 80 leg wheels (each leg)
> 30 Billy Daniels' pushups in 3 positions
> 60 leg raises
> 100 Lanciato exercises
> 130 Lanciato exercises (after rest)
> 30 leg raises with boots on
> 140 toe raises in 3 positions
> 50 leg raises
> 150 Lanciato exercises
> 110 Lanciato exercises (after rest)
> 30 leg raises
> 50 leg wheels

A few days later I ran to Bammental in 56 minutes, rested an hour, and ran back with Salter in 67 minutes.

On June 14 I received word from DiMarco who reported much snow on the Plateau Rosa, the track in the best shape ever. Competition would begin on July 20, a week later than in the past, and I was happy for the extra week to prepare.

I quit my job early in order to spend a few free days with my wonderful companion before leaving for Italy and skiing.

Journal, June 19, 1965:

I am full of good heart, anticipation of Cervinia and 100 mph. This year—the last for me—the goal is 180 kph. Good legs, good skis, a good tuck and much luck will tide me over while I learn myself again and test my courage and control. Other people would call it resolution, but that is a covering word and not exactly correct. I am in love with living today. Oh joy!

I had skied but a couple of times in five months and while my body was in excellent shape I needed skiing. It was time to go and I said goodbye to my black-haired, beautiful friend and went.

The first stop was San Pelligrino Terme near Bergamo for the first World Championship Slalom on plastic snow. San Pelligrino is known for its mineral water, but high above town was a good size hill covered with plastic mats and grass and serviced by lifts. La Piste del Sole was amazingly good skiing, though plastic requires different techniques than are used on snow. It was terrifically hot. The plastic was too hot from the heat until 5 p.m. when it was watered down and we all skied like mad for two hours in our swimming suits. The rest of the time we sat around the swimming pool in the sun. I couldn't get enough of it and I realized how much and deeply I missed the sun after a winter in Heidelberg.

Leo Lacroix, the great French skier, his brother, Guy, and Louis Jauffret were there from France. Adalbert Leitner, who raced for Austria but whose brother Ludwig raced for Germany, was there. Per Sunde, a medical student in Friberg, represented Norway. Joos Minsch of Switzerland was doing his first skiing since breaking his hips in Lauberhorn practice. There were some fine Italian skiers. We all enjoyed the pool and the sun as much as the skiing and it was a convivial time. Lacroix won the race and I fell, twice, an unpleasant experience on plastic.

Then Cervinia. I traveled there via a few good days of relaxation in Milano and Lago Como with my black-haired friend who met me in

Milano and left me in Cervinia.

Journal, June 25, 1965:

I have a ski bag for skis, a rucksack for boots, a handbag for books and a suitcase for clothes. Throughout the four are scattered miscellany and books that won't fit into the handbag. I am traveling much too heavy, it is not like in the 'old days.' Some people settle down when they get older, others just travel heavier.

Journal, July 2, 1965:

How one has arranged life for the third attempt at speed.

One gets up at seven, eats and reads and is at the lifts by 8. He goes up top, works an hour in exchange for lifts, skis until the lifts shut down at noon, works on the Lanciato track a little, and comes down for lunch. After lunch he reads until about 4:30 and then has an hour workout. He shaves in cold water and takes a sponge bath because there is no hot water here. He reads and writes until dinner and after dinner he goes to bed and reads until he falls asleep.

The sun is fierce and beautiful. I will never leave her again.

I ski the way arthritic spinsters must make love. That will change. It hurts too much to stay like this.

My boots and skis are marvelous.

The contour of the track is better than last year. It will be the toughest ever and I expect 180 will be broken or pressed.

My Lanciato exercises have helped but I still do not know if I can hold my head down. I feel strong, ambitious and tough. I do not know if I am becoming braver with age, more able to detach myself, of if I just don't care as much. As the spirit grows the importance of the body diminishes.

Shaving in cold water is not pleasant but it gives me a better shave. There is a moral in that.

When the Lanciato is over half my life is finished. There is a moral in that as well.

Much was different than in July 1964, only some of them were differences within me. I lived alone in a tiny hotel and took my meals with DiMarco. He was the same fine man but that just discernible shade overweight that made me know he had made a classic mistake of those who become yesterday's hero before their time. He was still the best technically and we practiced together and discussed for hours the next logical refinement of speed skiing—dropping the head between the knees for aerodynamic efficiency where vision is limited to feet and skis.

Journal, July 3, 1965:

I still ski like an arthritic lady but it is coming. In a week it should be here and I will be able to go to work.

I feel so sure of my ability to commit myself to speed. My greatest worry is keeping my head down. My position is much better than before, and the few trials I have made make me sure of holding it. The position and mental attitude I can hold, but holding the head down so you can't see at more than 100 mph is something else.....hoooooooowheeeeeeeemop!

Journal, July 4, 1965:

If there is sun tomorrow I will take up the 230s and have a go at the track. It is runable though not very good. I want to see how leaving the top buckles off my boots and keeping my head down works. We must start somewhere.

Knowing what I know now my hair stands on end to think what could be achieved in Chile with Luigi, a few others, people to prepare the track and man the watches, plenty of snow and a month of good weather. The first good day would see over 180, the possibilities are more....From now on every man who tries seriously and truly for a record carries death in his hind pocket. I think that this year everyone will make it, but after this it will get too fast, too tough, and eventually someone will but the farm no one ever wants but everyone gets.

Another difference was that through friends in the journalism business in Reno I had arranged that nothing about the speed run would appear in the Reno papers until it was over. It gave me more freedom and ability to concentrate if I did not have to worry about worrying my family.

Roberto Gasperl was back. He had worked in Aspen the preceding winter for Stein Eriksen and we had some good conversations about America, Stein, the Lanciato and the loss of peace and beauty to Cervinia and other places as more and more people filled them up. Roberto had not been training and was not planning to compete in the Lanciato.

Journal, July 5, 1965:

Today I ran twice with my 215s and the tops of my boots unbuckled. Tomorrow I take up the big skis and try from higher. The loose boots will take some getting used to.

A good workout this afternoon. Up the bobsled track and into the hills behind, stopping once for a round of calisthenics.

Journal, July 6, 1965:

Today was so good. Eight trips of about 130—140 kph and the good feeling of having it all come back on a perfect, beautiful day.

Journal, July 9, 1965:

When I get up in the morning and go up on the mountain I go to ski for myself and to prepare myself for the Lanciato, for what reasons I am not sure except that is seems the most important thing I have ever done. This will be the death of my competitive skiing, and the style and manner of death can sometimes be as important as those of life. Maybe that is why it seems so very important. After this I will be passé as a skier, even to myself. I will be a different person, especially to myself. And when I go up on the mountain I leave behind those parts of myself that do not ski for myself and run Lanciatos for what reasons they are not sure of.

In the morning I skied fresh powder when I was good and in wet snow when I was not. In between I worked hard on the track and had three runs which were perfectly composed and close to 100 mph. You can feel when the speed is more or less like that and of course you feel your position and composure. And tonight at dinner DiMarco paid me compliments on my runs. I am confident and strong and will try to use well the 10 days left of training.

The workouts after skiing stepped up, as did the amount and intensity of skiing. I ran about two hours each afternoon in the mountains above Cervinia, interspersed with complete sets of exercises each day. I enjoyed working like that, alone in the mountains with my entire concentration devoted to making myself the best Lanciato competitor possible. I was not abstracted, was paying very close attention to every detail of my simple and structured life, and I was in perfect physical condition for what I was doing. Mentally I was objective, spiritually I was there in that place I thought of as being at one with myself.

Journal, July 13, 1965:

Late afternoon of a most fantastic day. Up at the usual hour and skiing by 8:30. Two hours of hard skiing in the hot sun and four tries on the track from the top where it is steep. I was very good and I could feel it. Nothing matters except the times as they stand on the evening of July 25. That remains to be but I feel quite good about the Lanciato.

The next day Roberto Gasperl decided that he would, after all, compete in the Lanciato. I invited him to work out with me, but he was not in good shape and I had to finish alone.

Journal, July 14, 1965:

Bastille Day. 100 years ago Ed Whymper was the first man up the Matterhorn. Some others went up with him but they never made it back. The success of an endeavor is not the end of the story. It is the death of the impetus and, sometimes, only the beginning. Anyway, it's the anniversary of many things, among them Bastille Day. I hope all my French friends have a damn fine day.

For myself, unFrench as I am, it was still a good day. I skied well and had fun. I ran three times on the track. Each day I am stronger, more sure, in a better position and my head just a little lower.

Journal, July 15, 1965:

One is allowed to take a measure of contentment in the past tense, but true happiness is found in the present participle.

As soon as this race is over I must impose some stiff discipline upon my life. I must keep a mild workout schedule with more running than anything. I must review my manner of living and the necessities of life, for I have so much stuff in this room it looks like three men live here. There is something I don't like about having so much baggage, and it is something to do with the core of qualities

For the next two days weather didn't allow skiing. There was rain in the valley and snow on the mountain with wind. Winter in the summer Alps. I had flashes of the Portillo weather gods of 1963. The chance to rest was welcome, but any relief from the focus of attempt had to be handled skillfully. The edge had to remain sharp.

Journal, July 18, 1965:

Today was very good. At first it was too hard but later it softened. What the four of us who started high accomplished makes me feel sure a new record will be ours within a week. Alberti said we went 168. Egon with a hand watch said 167. I said above 165. Gasperl said very fast. And Luigi said veloce. Egon said that by his hand watch Bruno and I were the same, both faster than Luigi. I feel very strong and fast and like a hell of a guy today.

There is that nervousness and abstraction with which I am familiar. I am in very high spirits and I like to be with people I enjoy and not around people I don't like. It is a little bit as if I were someone else, though not so much as two years ago.

Messner, Stiegler and some others I like much are here. Good to talk to them. The Austrians go to Portillo on August 6. I would give much to go with them. Sometimes, when I long for another time and place, my thoughts go back to Chile. I am quite content here but I must move on in ten days or so.

The last day of practice was the fastest I had gone in Italy and I was confident. The weather was marginal.

Journal, July 19, 1965:

Tomorrow we begin for real. Today was about 170 kph. There is nothing more to do about any of it except hold the best position possible, hope for good snow, and have a drink of genepy as an offering to the Gods. I am as ready as I could or will ever be, and now we shall see. You and me.

CHAPTER SIX

Closing the circle

THE FIRST TIME IS A POWERFUL EXPERIENCE. No one ever really forgets their introduction to any facet of experience, though sometimes they would like to and other times they live in a suspended state of denial. Beginnings carry the pattern of the life to come as losing virginity signals the commencement of infinitely more than it ends, the start of another ring of beauty and life around your being. The beginning of something is like a song or poem and an unfinished song is just that.

The end of something is the closing of the ring, the completion of the circle, the beginning of another pattern and cycle. The first time is a powerful experience, the last one profound.

My first exposure to big speeds had been an emotional response to other experiences, a reaction to disappointment; but this time, the last time in big speeds, was a conscious choice. That is the difference between fate and freedom.

And Cervinia 1965 was the conscious finish to more than big speeds for me, ending a way of life I had pursued for 15 years, and I only had 26. I was ready to move on and there were no regrets, but I was acutely aware of death and birth, the old and the new, age and innocence, transcendence and transition. What had started on the slopes of tiny ski resorts around the shores of Lake Tahoe in California and Nevada at the beginning of the 1950s was ending on a giant track beneath the Matterhorn in the Italian Alps in the middle of the 1960s. On another level of awareness and American history it could be said that what came in on Korea was going out with Viet Nam, at least for those who see connections between an individual and his country. In between had been hundreds of starting gates, tens of thousands of miles, rivers of living, chasms of mistakes and a few bright stars of success, and, most important, everything I had.

All that I had attempted had not been accomplished, but I was acutely aware that it is the living attempt that keeps life alive and meaningful and evolving, and even within the particular, exotic facet of speed skiing, in which I had accomplished my best skiing moments and through which I was finishing competition, an entire cycle was nearly complete. The illusions with which I approached Portillo in 1963 had become by 1964 a lack of attention and loss of respect for my actions (for which I paid, by which I learned), and that had progressed by 1965 to a cold, objective, almost cynical view of preparation, competition and meaning in big speeds. The impetus for 1963 came from Ron Funk and I relied heavily on Ron's drive, taking courage and support from his spirit and our most worthy friendship which at this writing has given sustenance to us both for more than half a century. The next year in Cervinia I viewed C.B. and I as the Americans against all comers, record holders against the pack, patriots against the world. By 1965 I ran in Cervinia because I didn't want the rest of my life burdened with the fact of retiring on a broken leg and the inescapable questions my mind would have raised had I quit that way.

Like everyone, I had been becoming a different person all my life, and I was not the same as even so recently as 1964. My notes are full of the idea of living a different sort of life as soon as the Lanciato was finished.

If the 1965 Lanciato had gone off with nothing more untoward than the falls of 1964, the breaking of a record or the further development and revelation of personal character, which is one of the chief values of competition, my life afterwards would have likely taken a different direction than it did. But Cervinia 1965 was powerful and mind-expanding in ways I hadn't anticipated.

By 1965 the women's division had been eliminated and juniors competed with the men. There were more competitors from more countries, including national team members of Austria, Germany, Switzerland, Italy, Czechoslovakia. The one Finn was Kalevi, the one Australian was Georges Stock and I was the lone American. No one competed from Japan or France. There were 45 competitors, including many of the same friends and rivals from 1964—DiMarco, Siorpaes, Mussner, DeZordo, Plangger, DeNicolo, Messner, Mahlknecht and Agreiter. There were some new seekers of speed, a few well known from the racing circuit:

Ludwig Leitner of Germany, one of the world's best since 1960, world combined champion in 1964 and the leading downhill racer of 1965. Ludwig was a tough man.

Adalbert Leitner, Ludwig's brother who raced for Austria due to the unique geographical location of their home town.

Carlo Senoner, the often injured Italian who became world champion in slalom one year later in Portillo.

The Czech team, particularly Radim Kolousek and Janda Jaroslav, the leading skiers of their country.

Peter Rohr and Andreas Sprecher, the two best young Swiss.

Heini Schuler, a Swiss who had raced and coached in the American state of Washington. He worked for Head skis in Switzerland and came to Cervinia to coach Sprecher and Rohr. Heini decided to compete himself and beat his boys a few times. The Swiss and I lived in the same hotel and Heini and I had mutual friends in Washington and we became friends.

Gerardo Mussner, a cousin to Walter, and fast becoming one of the better downhill racers of the world.

There were many fine skiers in Cervinia that year and it was a bigger and more international competition than in 1964. Along with an expansion of fellowship and the competitive limits came a narrowing of the line of error.

A few days before competition began I rode down the cable car after practice with Walter Mussner. I had a strong instinctive liking for Walter, but he carried an abstract demeanor with him that had not been present at Christmas. We talked about our injuries of December and he told me he had been injured again later in the season. I asked about his conditioning for he appeared thin and more pale than before. This 19 year old boy who reminded me so much of Bud Werner and who I liked and who inspired good feelings just by his presence told me a terrible story: only a month before he was driving a car near Innsbruck and he was in a wreck that he said was his fault, and his father was killed. That is all I know about the wreck. Whatever the circumstances of the tragedy and wherever the blame, Walter carried the responsibility for it in his mind and heart. That is a heavy load and I was alarmed for this fine young person. It was evident that he could not possibly be either physically, mentally or emotionally prepared for what we were about to do, and I knew about not being prepared.

CHAPTER SEVEN

"Strange that we should think in straight lines, when there are none, and talk of straight courses, when every course, sooner or later, is seen to be making the sweep round, swooping upon the center. When space is curved, and the cosmos is sphere within sphere, and the way from any point to any other point is round the bend of the inevitable, that turns as the tips of the broad wings of the hawk turn upwards, leaning upon the air like the invisible half of the ellipse. If I have a way to go, it will be round the swoop of a bend impinging centripetal towards the center. The straight course is hacked out in wounds, against the will of the world."

D.H. Lawrence

JULY 20, 1965 WAS THE FIRST DAY OF COMPETITION and the first day is important; it sets the mood, determines pace and is the end of preparation. The weather that first day was not good—grey, warm and unstable. As before, the first run started low and I had 4th best time. The next round we moved up but the light was disappearing behind dark clouds. The track remained fast.

On the second round I completely lost position on the jump and finished with a struggling and thereby slow run, but I was strong and there was no terror. I managed 163.413 to tie for 13th. Luigi and Bruno tied for 1st with 169.252.

In 1964 the best first day time was 167 kph and second was 163. In

1965 four men were faster than 167 kph and fourteen faster than 163. I was not worried about my first day performance, though I was disappointed. I knew that losing my position had significantly slowed my run, and the large number of fast runs kept me optimistic about a record. Part of the reason for so many faster skiers was the improvement in body positions. Everyone was polishing and tightening. DiMarco led and everyone watched and heads were gradually coming down. The one disquieting factor was the wet and grim weather by the end of the day.

Results of the first ten, July 20, 1965

Bruno Alberti, Italy	169.252
Luigi DiMarco, Italy	169.252
Bruno DeZordo, Italy	169.014
Gerardo Mussner, Italy	168.460
Ludwig Leitner, Germany	166.821
Gildo Siorpaes, Italy	166.435
Kalevi Hakkinen, Finland	166.128
Alfred Plangger, Austria	165.745
Roberto Gasperl, Italy	165.137
Andraes Sprecher, Switzerland	164.458

July 21, 1965. The start list was dispensed with for some unannounced reason, but the competitors didn't figure this out until several late numbered racers were allowed to run out of order. This confusion (or assumption or lack of attention on my part) cost me the good track my starting order entitled me to on the first round. The weather was almost beautiful, the track deteriorating, but I had learned the lesson and was among the first to be ready for the second round, skis on, mind and body ready.

The track had been side-slipped between rounds and my second run was one of those free and magical experiences in which for a few moments time and space ceased to exist. I broke my tuck slightly off the jump but regained position immediately and in terms of feelings and the inner being it was a perfect run. My time was 165.435, third for the day behind Leitner and DiMarco.

By then it was obvious that Ludwig Leitner, easily the best downhill racer competing, was the only one who never varied his position through the jumps. His actual speed technique did not appear to my eye to be as good as that of several others, but he held it longer, steadier. On the second round he went 169.651, beating Luigi by 3 kph and me by 4.

Polishing and tightening continued. After talking with my coach, Egon Schopf, I realized my head was in good position but my butt was too low, creating an air drag below the horizontal, parallel to the track. As we discussed this and I prepared to go up for a third round the clouds moved in and the day was grey by the time I got on the lift. I was still riding up when Roberto Gasperl made his second run and I had an outstanding view of one of the most spectacular falls I've ever seen. Just before the jump it appeared to me that 'Robbie' caught an edge, though he later said he thought his ski came off. Either way, he was moving about 70 mph and went face first between his skis just where the hill begins to be steep. He fell end over end for more than a hundred meters and his body tomahawked with great speed and power. His fall took him through a marker disc, constructed of two 2x4s driven into the snow with a round piece of blue plywood nailed to the top. He shattered the posts and the disc into tiny pieces and he shattered his arm as well and then he stopped.

I noted in my journal that night:

When Robbie fell I was riding up the lift after my 2nd run. I saw the whole thing and afterwards he didn't move. I was full of fear for him and I kept saying to myself (or was it to myself?) "Please don't let him be dead. Don't let him die like that." I kept saying things like that and watching him not move a muscle. He is in much pain now and unhappy, but I was very relieved to know he only has a broken arm. I have visited him twice this afternoon in the First Aid building and he will be fine. He said to me, "Last year it was your turn, this year it is mine." I wondered if he knew how truly he spoke.

Though he was doing quite well I fear Robbie hadn't trained for this and his first mistake got him.

Leitner is too much.

Luigi is mad about being beaten today and about the track. The track really was very bad. Luigi himself was not at all bad, it is only that Leitner was and is too much.

I continued to the top. The clouds broke a little and we had word that Gasperl was not critically injured. I forced from my mind the image of him falling, and I concentrated on being able to keep my bottom slightly higher, head lower. The sun was out when I went for my 3rd run and it went well through the jumps and into the big speeds. I could feel the difference in raising my rear just a few inches, and I had a good run going, one of my best. Just as speed builds progressively to the end of the track, the condition of the track deteriorates in proportion to and because of that speed. The faster you go the harder you are on the track. On that run the track was the roughest I had ever experienced. About a hundred meters below the jumps I found myself thrown violently around a track that was a field of ruts and holes that would have been terrifying at half the speed. I came close—so very close—to skiing through the edge. My position exploded and I held on only with the strength of terror as I began to fall sideways to the right and backwards. My left ski came off the snow high enough that the tip was above my head. I should have fallen and the previous year I would have, but I was afraid to fall and all the hours of exercises and all the runs to Bammental and in the hills above Cervinia and the months of positive thinking and focus had given me an unusual strength, the strength to follow the wisdom of fear. I refused to fall and I somehow managed to get my ski back on the snow and my body into a semblance of stability before slamming into the transition. I am not sure why I didn't fall in the transition but I do know that I had an adrenalin fired strength of muscle that I had never known before.

The track was closed shortly after my run. I had a time of 163 (the fastest part of it on one ski), and I was happy competition was over for the day. I felt weak.

Results of the first eight, July 21, 1965

Ludwig Leitner, Germany	169.651
Luigi DiMarco, Italy	166.435
Dick Dorworth, USA	165.435
Walter Mussner, Italy	165.137
Bruno DeZordo, Italy	164.609
Peter Rohr, Switzerland	164.308
Gildo Siorpaes, Italy	164.001
Bruno Alberti, Italy	163.562

Journal, July 22, 1965:

The weather and the track were not good enough to allow running today, but we did a lot of waiting. I made the officials mad when I told them the piste hadn't had enough work. I had gone up quite early, before they arrived, to look at the track. They had not packed it yesterday afternoon. They had only side-slipped it and had not taken time to fill in the holes and they had left big ridges of snow which had frozen solid. I told them it was ridiculous to expect people to ski at 100 mph on such a track. I did not know the word for inconsiderate, which is sconsiderato, or I would have mentioned that it is also that. Above all, it is dangerous. They are quite mad at me because I said their track is no good and they said it is perfect. Anyway, nothing was good enough to try today and so the track wasn't tested to see if it was perfect or malissimo and tested at the expense of some competitor's well being.

But we have lost a day and the weather is still horrible and I do not now anticipate the record going. We need good snow and for good snow we need sun and cold nights, and all we get is bad weather and cold all the time. Right now it is raining steady and hard. Every rain has its own character and this rain, Cervinia rain, July 22, 1965 rain, is frustrating.

Ma, domani e un altro giorno.

I want more than I have ever wanted anything in skiing the one run I know is there with head down, butt up and the snow the way it should be. That's what I want by Sunday.

Journal, July 23, 1965

No matter what they say, a day is not like any other day. No matter what they say. Today, for instance: after two runs I was at 160, 5 kph behind Leitner who was first and in about 7th or 8th place. The track was bad as well as slow and it wasn't getting any better. I held my position on the jump and lost it on the bad track both times, so I decided I'd learn from my third run of the other day and leave. I left. About five minutes later a cloud covered the sun for about 10 minutes and about 20 people went over 160, some of them over 165. Alberti is first with 167 and Sperotti is right behind him. I was wrong to leave and, instead of learning from the other day, I hurt myself.

More and more this becomes a competition between men and not an attempt at speed. There are too many competitors and the track is never in shape. Weather does not help.

There are two more days and it only takes one run, but you weren't very good in there today, Boy.

Tonight the German and Japanese movies of last year's Kilometro Lanciato will be shown. It will be fun to sit in a movie house in good health and watch myself break my leg.

I am very tired of sponge baths and washing my hair from a bucket. I need and want and yearn for a shower. Sunday I will have a bath or a shower somewhere, somehow, someway, something.

Results of first ten, July 23, 1965

Bruno Alberti, Italy	167.597
Antonio Sperotti, Italy	167.286
Walter Mussner, Italy	166.666
Sepp Heckelmiller, Germany	165.669
Peter Rohr, Switzerland	165.669
Bruno DeZordo, Italy	165.517
Luigi DiMarco, Italy	165.441
Ludwig Leitner, Germany	165.365
Radim Kolousek, Czechoslovakia	165.289
Renzo Zandegiacomo, Italy	165.213

Journal, July 24, 1965:

Another day lost to the weather Gods. It wasn't even worth going up on the cable car. The officials have decided to extend the race another day, to the 26th, but the snow is bad and weather unimproved and everything seems anticlimactic. There are two days left but we would all be surprised to see anyone go over 170. Luigi and I will see if Kneissl will send us to Portillo. I doubt that he will, but I do not like to end on a note of anti-climax.

Plangger has already gone and I fear some of the others will follow. There is nothing to be done about it, but I am good at meeting a challenge and I am good at relaxing afterwards, and I am not good at this thing of doing nothing. Waiting. Frustration. Especially when I have had but one good run in three days. We must wait.

Today I wrote and read. I took a walk with Robbie Gasperl and had lunch with Luigi. In awhile I'll workout and then I will read some more and wait for tomorrow. I do not know what I would do without good books. The anti-intellectual might answer "something constructive," and he may be right, but I would not enjoy it so much and I would not have enough time left over to do the other things like skiing. Good books enrich and nourish while productive activity (I do not mean work) only keeps people from doing what they want, both good and bad.

My main worries after the next two days are the weather being good so I can climb the Matterhorn and to find a job next winter so I can ski. I must be very careful not to get sidetracked into a city or a real job for the winter. I must write to justify it all and because that is what I want to do, and I must ski because it makes me happy. Any other good graces are different flavors of frosting.

Journal, July 25, 1965:

It is a Sunday afternoon and Cervinia is crowded. More crowded this year than last. People even walk in groups in the street and sing which is nice to hear, but it is raining and how can people sing when it is raining? Especially today. I do not understand how people can sing today. I do, really, but to hear people singing in the street reminds me of my own inability to sing today.

The weather was better than yesterday. Good enough to entice us up to the Plateau Rosa but not good enough to allow us up the ski lifts to the track. We waited a long time and I had a good talk with Heini Messner and I enjoyed that. Afterwards, Rivetti and Franca and the girl living with Franca who is Mussolini's niece and Zanni and Paolo and I came down and ate cheese and drank wine in the Funivie Station. That was fun and I like these people. Then I came down to the hotel and changed and went to look for a newspaper. On the way I saw a girl going the other way whom I had once met. It was raining and she had an umbrella and she asked me where I was going and I told her and she came with me and protected me from the rain with her umbrella. She even walked me clear back to the hotel with her umbrella after there was no paper to buy.

Yesterday I had a bath at Franca's. A long, hot, incredibly enjoyed bath, the first in nearly a month. When it was over I had a beer with Franca and Paolo and Mussolini's niece and I told them how wonderful was my bath and that I was a new man. Today I must have looked glum, for Mussolini's cute niece said that maybe I'd better have another bath for I was no longer a new man. I said no, I felt very old right then.

And my climb up the Matterhorn does not seem likely. Two men fell yesterday, one was killed. The guides blame it on too much snow and it is not likely I will find one to take me up. Not for a few weeks. Maybe I will be forced to go to the seashore. "And afterwards everyone goes to the seashore." That is not a bad theme. It becomes more enticing all the time. Dassin had a good idea there, and the honest whore is more profound that the bitch Phaedra.

Journal, July 29, 1965:

Heidelberg. Afternoon. I do not feel like writing. I cannot read. I do not feel like anything. I was wrong to think we would get by this year with everyone alive, and on Monday Walter Mussner went out the hardest way. I do not feel like writing, but I must put here about Walter, July 26th, the Lanciato and death while they are as vivid and fresh as they are right now.

The morning of the 26th the track was ice down to the blue disc (the one

Gasperl hit), about 100 meters above the trap. Solid, wind-blown ice. Below that the track was covered with soft, new snow, about eight inches deep, blown there by the laws of terrain and wind. Those in charge prepared it in the same masterly fashion. We were two days without skiing and this day was added to the schedule, it was an extension of our time. We went up to the Plateau Rosa early. The weather was beautiful, a slight bit cold.

At the top we joked, wished each other luck, did warm up exercises, adjusted equipment—just like always. I was completely absorbed in what had to be done. The two days off skis were noticeable.

Mussner went first. His time came back up as 172.084. I was really excited when I heard that. The first time over 170 this year! The record was in sight! I ran 5th or 6th and held my position. It was a wonderful, free run, but I felt the change going off the ice onto soft snow. My time was 170.373, but I, and everyone else on the outrun, thought they announced 173. I hurried back up thinking I had the best run of the round, and I was full of getting the record back. I don't know what it is about that bloody record.

When I got to the top Ninni told me I was 4th behind Mussner, Siorpaes and Leitner. That seemed logical because I had been surprised to hear my time as 173. It hadn't felt so fast. The slight disappointment filled me even more with desire for the record. I kept saying to myself, "I'm gonna get that bastard back." I talked a little with Mussner and congratulated him for his fine first run. I spoke to Siorpaes. I observed the rituals. I remember grinning because I was sure Mussner and Siorpaes were as full of the record as I.

Then there came a time when no one wanted to go. There was no particular reason. One hadn't finished waxing. Another was cold. Still another was tuning his mind. I was still tired from climbing up too fast. Mussner appeared ready abut he didn't want to go, I don't know why—nerves probably. (I'm sure now he had a premonition.) I jumped into the breach and said I was ready. Actually, I was still tired, but I was so excited and anxious about finally breaking into the 170s that it didn't matter. I went anyway and I held my position over both jumps. I put my head down just before the soft part of the track, and immediately pulled it back up. The track was a monstrous mess. It hadn't even been side-slipped between rounds. I lost my position. It was like driving a car across a furrowed field at 100 mph.

I didn't know how fast it was but I knew it wasn't very good. Now I know that my time was 168.539 kph. I was mad about the track and I skied to a stop in front of Egon. I said, "The track is really bad, Egon, why don't they work on it?" He knew what I meant and felt just about like I did and he said something like, "I don't know. You can't talk to these fucking Italians. Then I said, quote, "Well, someone's going to get hurt up there." Unquote.

Egon took my skies and began waxing them. A few were still getting into the 170s and I was full of—with luck—the record.

Then Mussner came.

On Sunday night, the 25th, Mussner saw a photo of Luigi taken on the first day. In this photograph Luigi's head is completely down and all you can see is the top of his helmet. It is the most fantastic Lanciato photo I've seen. Walter studied the photograph for a few minutes. "Tomorrow I will do that," he told Luigi. Luigi grinned as any champion will whose disciples are trying to imitate him. It is the grin of pride and of being flattered, but it is also a grin of awareness of the difficulties in the refinements of any champion's technique, the refinements which all disciples try for and hardly any ever achieve. In this case, the refinement of putting one's head between one's knees and skiing blind at more than 105 mph.

Mussner came and his head was down. I have the impression that when I was on top and Walter didn't want to go he was forcing himself to be able to put his head down. (Perhaps also fighting a premonition.) This is what I think but there is no way to know. Later, Franca told me that Mussner nearly didn't go again. I don't know why, not does anybody. Then he said something like, "Well, there's still the record," and he left the top.

He came and I saw him from above the blue disc, just before where the track was bad. His head was already down, his position was good, and he held it like that all the way. Many things went into the sequence of what happened then and no one will ever know exactly what they were, but this is what I think:

At the top of the timing area he began to veer right. I saw immediately that he was on his way off the track. A cold electric shock passed through me like a tidal wave of fear. My heart went numb and my blood disappeared.

Walter went off the track just at the end of the timing, just missing the electric eye pillar. He went through a little post and that ridiculous net they had fanned out on each side. When he hit that post the world changed.

At that speed many things could cause a slight deviation of direction. It is impossible to have more than an opinion as to why he went off the course. It was obvious from watching how he held his position, and from what he said afterwards, that he was unaware he was off course until he had already fallen. I believe two things killed Walter Mussner, not one more than the other. I think the bad track caused him to veer to one side against the natural slope of the track, and I think Walter's head being down made him unaware of what was happening, and, therefore, unable to correct it. I think if the track had been properly groomed he wouldn't have veered off course, and if he had kept his head up he would have known what was happening and would have been able to correct it. But—and Walter Mussner is dead.

What happened when Walter hit that post and fell is something I don't think I will forget as long as I live, and it will be more than a few days before the image leaves my mind, allowing me easy sleep at night and to write and read and be naturally of this life the rest of the time. He clocked a time of 170.132 kph just as he fell, but to the naked eye it appears that the racers in the last 30 meters of the 100 meter trap accelerate to a much greater speed. I would not be surprised if the racer who clocks 170 for 100 meters is traveling at 190 for the last 10 or 20 meters. Right there, where there is that little boost of acceleration that anyone can observe, Walter fell. With incredible force and speed he went end over end, feet and then head hitting the snow, and each turn wrenching his body unbelievably. Afterwards, eleven holes were counted in the snow, feet, head, feet, head, feet, head, and, at the end, everything. It was difficult to believe it was a human body undergoing such gyrations, such speed, such force. The only thing I have ever seen like it were movies of Bill Vukovich's car at Indianapolis when he was killed in 1955. It was similar to that.

For a few seconds that seemed like minutes after he stopped in a motionless pile in the transition everyone was frozen still with astonishment and fear. There was—I am sure in everyone because it was there in me—the hope of a miracle that Walter Mussner would get up and that no one would have to go pick him up. At the same time, I don't think there was a doubt in anyone's mind that he wasn't going to move by himself. I have seen some bad falls and I have even had a few myself, but this wasn't like a skiing fall anyone had ever seen before. No one has ever fallen like that.

Then Rico was screaming over the loudspeaker. That snapped people out of their trance. Dozens of people were suddenly all around Walter, about 30 yards from where I stood. I started to go but instinct told me not to and I'm glad I didn't. Ivo (Mahlknecht) and Felice (DeNicolo) were there and they were closer comrades than I, so he wasn't alone when he shouldn't be alone.

It took about half an hour to get him off the hill. During that time not one person even side slipped the track, though competition was obviously to continue as soon as possible. I was mad and sick with the knowledgeable suspicion that if Walter wasn't dead he was an agonizing pile of broken bones. Egon was furious the way the German temperament gets furious when unhappy.

I stared at the group around Walter. Egon finished waxing my skis. I was, however, finished psychologically and spiritually, and I knew it. I told Egon I would run again if the track began to be fast enough for a record. I would go up and wait and listen to the times. If they got close I would go, if not, not. Egon said it was finished but I went up and waited anyway, but I never came down on the track.

Just before I went up to wait Hans Berger broke away from the group around Walter and came my way. Hans, who lives in Kufstein, is small with tiny, delicate features and an expressive face. He usually looks about 18 years old, though he is 30. When he came up to me he looked a hundred years old and there were tears in his eyes.

"Ist es schlecht?" I asked.

"Ja," he said in a strange way.

"Sehr schlecht?"

"Sehr schlecht," he answered in a way that made me know it was.

I went up to the top and waited with that in the pit of my stomach. Probably it was best the track never got fast enough to make me think a record was possible.

They took Walter to Aosta and he lived a little more than five hours. Unfortunately, he was conscious most of that time. He fractured his skull, broke two vertebrae in his neck, pulverized his entire pelvic region, broke one femur and tore himself open from the anus to the navel. He had acute hemorrhages of the brain, stomach and leg. Toward the end he went blind. If he had lived he would have lost one leg, he wouldn't have been a man any longer, and he probably would have been paralyzed. Kiki went with him to Aosta and held his hand until he died. She is only twenty and had never seen a dead person before, and she was still in shock and sometimes hysterics the next night when she and her mother told me about it.

The Italian and Swiss papers are full of stupid things about it. The people of Cervinia all say that the track was 'perfetto' and they put the whole blame on a mistake of Walter's. they've gone on at some length why it's not the fault of Lanciato committee, the organization or anyone's. That is not quite true. Some say there's nothing dangerous about the Lanciato. That, too, is not quite true. Others call the Lanciato stupidly insane. Nor is that true. If I uttered to the press what I think about the track they would interpret it as blaming those responsible for track maintenance for Walter's death. That, also, is not the truth, and it would do infinitely more harm than good. And it would not help Walter. There is no prevention (except abstinence which is ridiculous) for such accidents and there is no blame. It is part of skiing that fast.

I was the only one competing that day who saw Walter fall and I returned to the top with a different perspective on our endeavors. The racers and officials asked about the delay. Why was the track closed so long? I said Walter had a fall that tore up the track a bit, the delay was necessary for repairs. I had neither desire nor right to elaborate.

I sat at the top for a long time. Some racers got in six runs, nearly everyone got in four or five. Only Mussner and I ran just twice. Visions of his fall tumbled through my brain. I could not make them leave. (They entered my dreams and woke me in the night for the next two years.) It was the same clear day but a grainy, colorless filter had descended on the world.

Leitner, leading with 172.744, decided not to run again unless his time was beaten. It never was. My time dropped from fourth best to eighth. Luigi, suffering badly from a strep throat and cold, took five runs before breaking into the first ten. My place on the result sheets, the race itself, winning or losing no longer mattered. What importance has the race alongside life itself? What game do we play in which the loser forfeits life? What type of men play this game? For it was obvious from the beginning that one of us would die because of some human failing, neglecting for a billionth of eternity the rules of the game. Is human failure cause to die? If it is, are we not playing with the rules and stakes of Neanderthal Man? I never meant to play a game in which one of the players would inevitably, through mathematical laws as sure as those governing Russian Roulette, smash his body beyond repair; yet I played and watched it happen and I felt deep in my innards that I had always known it was going to happen. I remembered waiting for C.B. at the bottom of Portillo's track, wondering about the game's next move if he beat my time. The questions would not disappear. I had no answers.

My friend Franca Simondetti gave Leitner and I some Sangria. We drank it over small talk and silence. Strange to drink the sweet Sangria, to feel its wonderful vapors fill your body and your brain, exploding your taste buds as you sit in the sun—sweet Sangria—all the while trapped with death in a vision of the boyish face of Walter Mussner and a fall unlike any other. Strange to sit like that with Ludwig Leitner, the big German who exudes toughness and confidence and plays the game hard, drinking and healthy. Life's mysteries unfold through everyday functions.

Tiring of Sangria, small talk and waiting for a run I neither wanted nor would ever make, I skied down alongside the track. Racers were still coming, about one a minute. As a competitor I was allowed to stand close to the track, and I watched big speeds from about 30 feet away. For the first time in three years of playing with eternity I viewed it with a new realization of flesh and blood men, mere mortals, at play with the forces of the universe; it was wondrous that we dared, but never again would I view another man as a rival whose mistakes or refinements I must note and use to my advantage. I could hardly believe what I saw. I knew these men. We had joked, laughed, ate, drank and skied together. We had entered into freedom and struggled with terror, and together we had ignored our common reality. Walter Mussner reminded us of our negligence. I watched my friends like children in a play yard, proud, arrogant, innocent. We had accomplished great things, but when all was done and spoken we were just men; probably we could be better men, for we had not put away childish things.

When I was 12 years old my parents sent me away to a Christian Brothers boarding school for boys in Sacramento, California. After six weeks, in one of the first—and best—independent decisions of my life, I ran away from the school and phoned my folks to let them know. My father came from Tahoe to get me and he threatened to return me to the school. I told him that if he did that I would run away again and next time I wouldn't phone him. We both knew that I meant it. Dad, a kind and gentle man for the most part, was furious in the way that complicated dilemmas of life make all of us furious sometimes, and he berated me and said things to and about me that a father should not say to a son and I began crying. My tears only added to his frustration with me and infuriated him even more. Dad ridiculed me and told me that I was a 'baby' and I felt so very bad that I managed to quit crying and wipe away my tears. Being called a baby by the man I most loved was the ultimate insult, and I badly did not want to ever be known as a baby.

And for the next 14 years I only cried one other time, a few months earlier when my beautiful aunt Llewellyn died. And all those years and miles and sadnesses and joys away from my father's thoughtless if understandable venting of his frustration on my childhood, I stood by the Kilometro Lanciato speed track watching men ski like jet crusaders on the devil's tail, and I badly wanted to cry. I was filled with grief but I had forgotten how to cleanse myself with tears. The sorrow was deep and clear within me but it could not get out past the defenses I had built so that the world would never view me as a baby. It is not too much to posit that speed skiing itself was a part of that structure. I watched my friends and fellow competitors and I was inexpressibly sad and profoundly ashamed.

When I got down to Cervinia the word was around that Walter was badly hurt. Only those who saw him fall or who were with him after had any idea what that meant. Most of the racers didn't think that Walter would not be back with them. I returned to my hotel, changed clothes and packed my ski bag for Egon to take to Kufstein. Walter was in Aosta and I had heard that he was alive when he reached the hospital, usually a good sign for the chances of survival. I put my thoughts with Walter Mussner and packed my bag.

After, I was carrying the heavy bag of skis up the street to Egon's hotel when something happened I cannot define but only describe. It came in what I have come to know as a 'flash.' Suddenly I knew Walter Mussner was dead. It was sure. It was something I knew. Walter was dead and I no longer felt the hard sadness that had been with me since the fall. What I felt was something like intense peace and joy and relief, all together. I do not know if that feeling arose because Walter was out of his suffering, or because what had happened had happened to him and not to me, or if there was another reason. I set down my big, red Kneissl ski bag and rested. I did not question the fact of his death nor the quality or means of my knowledge, but I wasn't supposed to feel what I felt. For I felt better and more alive than I had since Walter began veering right.

An hour later Kalevi told me Walter Mussner was dead.

Journal, July 4, 1965:

From now on every man who tries seriously and truly for a record carries death in his hind pocket. I think that this year everyone will make it, but after this it will get too fast, too tough, and eventually someone will buy the farm no one ever wants but everyone gets.

I was wrong, of course, to think or at least to write that I thought "...that this year everyone will make it." In the same way and for very much the same reasons that I could not cry when filled with sorrow and unshed tears, reassuring myself in the privacy of my journal that this year everyone will make it was another defense against the reality of what we were doing with our lives, or, at least, another defense against acknowledging and accepting responsibility for the inescapable consequences of that reality.

And this is the identical defense constructed by modern man and his civilizations to pretend that this year everyone will make it through linear thought and talk of straight courses when, as Lawrence pointed out, "The straight course is hacked out in wounds, against the will of the world."

. . . .

Dick Dorworth